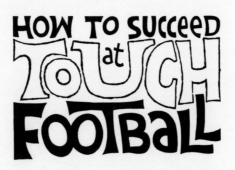

HOW TO SUCCEED at TOUCH FOOTBALL

by Frederic A. ☆☆☆ ☆BIRMINGHAM

☆ ☆

illustrated by Robert Osborn

THE MACMILLAN COMPANY
MACMILLAN NEW YORK, LONDON

© *Frederic A. Birmingham* 1962

The Macmillan Company, New York
Collier-Macmillan Canada Ltd., Galt, Ontario

PRINTED IN THE UNITED STATES OF AMERICA

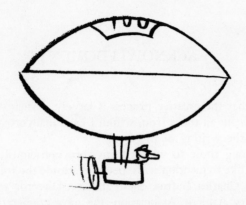

Introduction

The <u>time</u>: Sometime last spring
The <u>place</u>: A publisher's office
The <u>cast</u>: A publisher, an author, an artist

<u>Publisher</u>:   I'd like to introduce you two fellows. Mr. Osborn, this is Mr. Birmingham. Mr. Birmingham, Mr. Osborn.

<u>Birmingham</u>:   Hello, Osborn.

<u>Osborn</u>:   Hi.

<u>Publisher</u>:   All right, let's cut out the palaver and get the book out.

ACKNOWLEDGMENTS

In that the creative process is largely derivative, I should like to thank all those from whom I have inadvertently filched ideas in the writing of this book.

Among those to whom I am very consciously indebted, I should like to mention with special gratitude the following:

Mr. Charles Loftus, the Publicity Director of the Yale University Athletic Association; the most cooperative and informed man on the intercollegiate scene;

General John V. Grombach, the Walter Camp of Touch Football, whose magnanimous suggestions in his chosen field helped in so many ways;

Lt. Col. Fred E. Steele III, officer, teacher, and staunch ambassador of Touch;

The U.S. Army Infantry School Library, Fort Benning, Georgia;

The New York Public Library, for inestimable courtesies and research information;

Mr. Robert Osborn, for appreciative chortles over the long-distance telephone as each bit of manuscript came creeping in to his drawing board;

Miss Mimi Hogan, typist extraordinary, who suffered a grievous slump in her social life as this manuscript was being converted from scribbles into something a printer might deign to scan;

Mr. Robert Markel, my editor, who intermixed eternal vigilance and patience in a continuously encouraging brew;

My wife Frances, pass catcher of weekend Touch, who stifled her curiosity and never asked to see the manuscript until it was done, and then sensibly refrained from comment; and,

My father, who, Edwardian moustaches, goatee, and all, was the best passer I ever saw.

F.A.B.

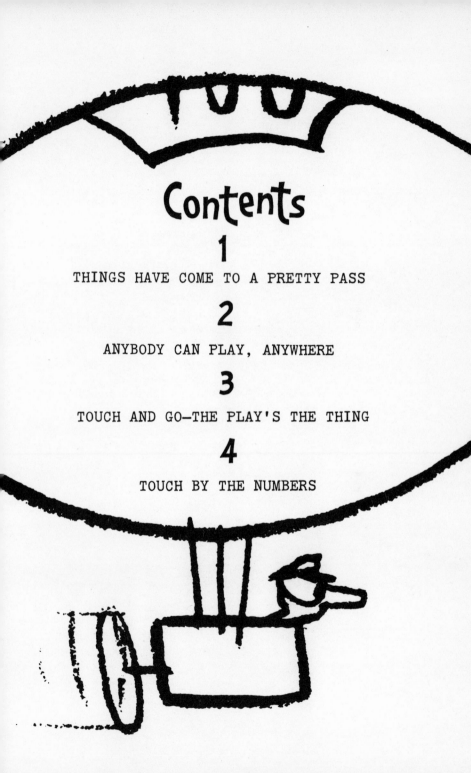

Contents

Things Have Come
to a Pretty Pass

ALL PATRIOTIC AMERICANS WILL RECOGNIZE THE TRUTH OF A
RUMOR THAT WHEN MRS. JACKIE KENNEDY RETURNED FROM
her junket to India, the President solicitously inquired if
her hosts were playing real or touch polo.

It was at that precise moment in time, according to the
purists in such matters, that Touch Football—to be known
hereinafter as "Touch," according to the In crowd—
achieved its status as America's most affectionately regarded
sport. It was at that moment, also, that the bulk of other
organized sports took off on the long downhill grade which

will culminate in their ultimate extinction, probably sometime about A.D. 2000.

In their place, as any schoolboy and most political ob-
servers can see, Touch will reign. It is the game of the fu-
ture, if not of the immediate present, for back and front
yards, for side streets, for corner lots, for lawns adjacent to
houses—fraternity, sorority, suburban, and White. Some
three hundred Yale students yearly play Touch in a league
composed of teams representing their twelve residential colleges, the undergraduate segment of the University. And
these colleges all play their equivalents from Cambridge,
Massachusetts, on the weekend of the Harvard-Yale game
of regular football. Out on the West Coast, those playing
on regular teams number more than 100,000, and another
half million untouchables draw up tag lines anywhere and
anytime they can. Staten Island has its own League, com-
plete with uniforms and shock troops skilled in pulverizing
the opposition without resorting to sissy tactics such as
tackling. Leonard Lyons, the doughty columnist of the
New York Post, has been pictured in the Sport section of
Time magazine, hotfooting it after one of his four sons in
a fast game of Touch. His greensward in Central Park
has also been trampled by Ralph Bunche, top U.N.'er, and
Phil Silvers, top banana. And, of course, at Hyannis Port,
Massachusetts, in Washington, D.C., and in its assorted sub-
urbs, the Kennedy clan has made Touch the symbol of the
New Frontier, with its borders extending to the infinite.
During the President's tumultuous welcome in Mexico
City, one local moppet held up a sign saying: "We play
touch football too."

There's a thing about Touch, too, which is more than
merely social. If you enjoy falling down, and are too lazy

" . . . Real or touch polo?"

to do it for yourself, then take up boxing or regular football. But Touch has the physical therapy without the traction that comes afterwards. Even the big boys in the professional football leagues tacitly admit this by playing Touch as often as they can. My friend Bob Teague, the brilliant young sportswriter of *The New York Times*, and himself an ex-Wisconsin backfield star, backs this up with a playful tale. Reports Bob:

In their final workout before most of their games in the National Football League, the New York Giants divide themselves into from four to six touch-football teams. It is a form of relaxation and fun that the coaching staff approves, since it helps to relieve pregame tensions.

During one such frolic on the Fordham University practice field last season, Y. A. Tittle, the team's regular quarterback, invented a sure-fire scoring play. Playing right end (all players were at unfamiliar positions), Tittle played hooky from his team's huddle and hid behind a stack of lumber in front of the bleachers, off the field. When his team snapped the ball, Tittle emerged from his hiding place, received a long wobbly pass from a lineman-turned-quarterback and walked unmolested into the end zone. The play covered about 55 yards. Upon crossing the end line, Tittle doffed his red baseball cap, revealing his bald head, and bowed in a courtly manner. It counted as a touchdown, of course. The Giants are more interested in having fun than in obeying rules during these carefree sessions.

Touch is an old game, but up until now, it has been the special possession of the Out crowd—nonvarsity athletes, intramural undergraduate heroes, small boys, and puffing fathers trying to get through to Junior.

But now the Kennedys have given the game a new

cachet. When an elderly Senator advises a fledgling newcomer to the Washington scene, "Get in Touch," he means just what he says. It's The Thing To Do.

The metamorphosis of Touch is a fascinating study. Part of its new shine is even attributable to an ancient American yearning. When we won the Revolution, we lost a king, and have regretted that vacancy, at least, ever since. We don't really want a ruling king, anymore than Great Britain does, but we'd like one to play with, like Monaco's. It is preposterous, of course, to imply that any President of the United States has any kingly significance. But the laying on of a Kennedy hand over a football, recalls the traditional rite of British kings, as their Touch became a guarantee for the banishment of scrofulous taint.

Right now, Touch is the least scrofulous thing in the U.S.

No *pronunciamentos* have accomplished this. But the thing is done. For example, in the same week in which Attorney General Robert Kennedy celebrated Memorial Day by joining U.S. Supreme Court Judge "Whizzer" White (an ex-all American footballer himself) in a game of Touch, the U.S. State Department fielded a baseball team against a nine from the Japanese Embassy, with Ambassador Koichiro Asakai himself playing first base. This was admittedly a vast improvement over Pearl Harbor, and was dutifully reported in the public press. The concurrent game of Touch was not reported in the papers, but the details were nevertheless known to The Right People. It is clear that baseball is for the Outs: Touch is In.

Touch, therefore, is both chic and important on the modern scene, exemplifying another highly rated Kennedy trait, pronounced *vigah*, already appreciated in sensitive

centers such as Moscow, Berlin, Paris, and London.

Is it too much to hope that some day Touch may be the means of solving diplomatic impasses? I don't know about Nikita's accuracy, but Jack is acknowledged to have the best throwing arm in the Kennedy family. It might be worth a try. Jack and his brother Bobby versus Khrushchev and Gromyko.

There are other possibilites, too, broadly hinted at by none other than the redoubtable Mr. Jimmy Hoffa, not otherwise distinguished as a devotee of Ivy League relaxations.

It came about that my friend George Tames, who heads up the Washington photo bureau of *The New York Times*, and who is one of the "regulars" in the Bobby Kennedy axis of Touch players who drift rapidly over the Washington landscape, was shooting Hoffa on assignment. To pleasant up the moment, George remarked that he planned to be playing Touch that same weekend with a friend of Jimmy's. By name, one Robert Kennedy, Chief Investigator of the McClellan Congressional Committee, then casting a chary eye on Union practices.

Mr. Hoffa's steady eyes took on a dreamy glow.

Quoth he: "I'd give a thousand dollars to get into that game."

We can never be sure that Mr. Hoffa's fervent wish was motivated exclusively by a desire for wholesome exercise. But it brings out another point about Touch—its strong amateur bias. It is a game by invitation only. Mr. Hoffa never did face Mr. Kennedy on the field of Touch.

The appearance of Touch on the New Frontier is personified by a familiar Monday morning phenomenon on the Washington scene. A number of otherwise well-set-up and carefully groomed gentlemen in their mid-thirties appear in the capital's most influential offices wearing an expression of controlled suffering, intermixed with slight overtones of grandeur. They move carefully and slowly, as if walking on eggs and hoping to crush as few as possible. Their everyday gestures, such as pointing or sitting down, are performed with unwonted care, and an occasional twitch. All in all, they appear to be held together on this particular A.M. by wires—or perhaps just by pride.

It is a good guess that any such gentlemen you encounter are not recovering from recent minor surgery, but from a Touch of stiffness. They are part of Bobby Kennedy's unlisted club, which gathers to toss a few as informally as they might drift out on the campus on any college to while away a couple of vigorous hours.

Word of a forthcoming game just gets around. The

boys meet by accident, perhaps at lunchtime at The May-
flower, or they pick up the phone and make a few calls
on Thursday evening, and there's a pretty good showing
by the time Sunday afternoon rolls around. The meeting
hour is about 1 P.M., allowing for family and social chores
before and after. Bobby Kennedy is the leading spirit, but
Ethel Kennedy may show from time to time, or even the
President himself if he can get away—to the barely con-
cealed horror of the Secret Service, as he leaps high to snare
a pass, or takes a tumble as he misses one.

They formerly gathered on the football field of the
American University, simply taking to the turf without
any preliminaries such as asking permission, just like any
urchins looking for a place to play catch. They were eventually kicked off this field by a gentleman who revealed
himself as the President of the University and whose con-
viction that they had no right to be there was unmoved
by the news that some of the interlopers ranked high in the
Administration.

A rock-ribbed sward in Georgetown was their next
home, but eventually they found their way to Western
High School, in Bethesda, Maryland, where they currently
play. They have two adjacent fields to use, if they want,
and one is marked out for football. The area is fresh and
open, rimmed with trees, and a pleasant place to exchange
cares of government for the action and camaraderie of
Touch.

Bobby Kennedy is the spark plug of the outfit, playing
his favorite role of quarterback with characteristic ferocity
and single-mindedness. This is no soft bunch of dilettantes,
Monday morning Charley horses to the contrary. They
bang into the game with the zest of the New Frontier,

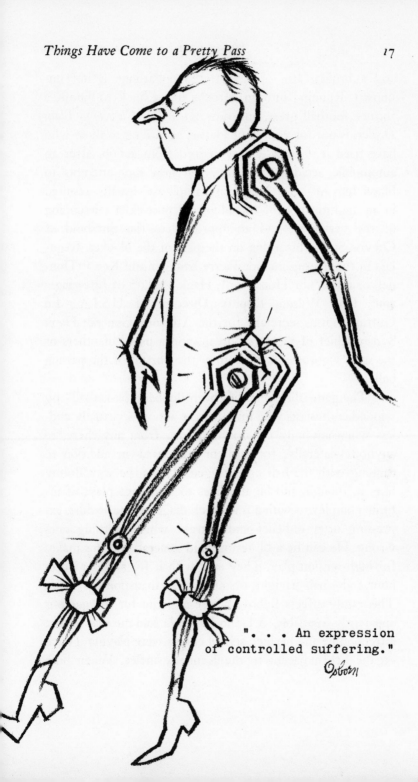

"... An expression of controlled suffering."

Osborn

and a broken arm or a shattered collarbone is not unknown. Running into an aurochs like Chuck Molinoff, a
former football great, and now with *The Cleveland Plain
Dealer*, is not for your aunt Hattie, according to those who
have tried it. Chuck is now retired from action, after an
automobile accident. But they tell how any attempts to
block him off—in a Mencken paraphrase—usually resulted
in an agglutination of the blood corpuscles, a telescoping
of the vertabrae, and an approach to the threshold of
Cheyne-Stokes breathing on the part of the blocker. Regulars in the line-up include Pierre Salinger and Ken O'Don-
nell of the White House staff; Hank Walker of *Life* magazine; Don Wilson, Deputy Director of U.S.I.A.; Ed
Guttman, press secretary for the Attorney General; Hank
Sydan, Chief of the *Life* bureau; and a passel of others of
the same vigorous ilk who enjoy the pursuit of the passing
ball.

The game they play has been dubbed "basketball" by
winded enthusiasts who find that the action is virtually end-
less when anybody can pass anytime, from anywhere, to
anybody—laterally, forward, or backward—in addition to
running with the ball until tagged. That's the way Bobby
likes it, though, and he also likes to introduce plays of infinite complexity with a few quick diagrams in the dust, ex-
pressing utter disbelief and outrage when anything goes
wrong. He can be a blistering field general, and this makes
for high-tension play. They stay with it for an hour or an
hour and a half straight, or until semi-exhaustion has set in.
This rarely affects Bobby, whose appetite for the game is
apparently insatiable. A lad in Bethesda told me that on one
afternoon he and his high school chums were playing Touch
on the field adjacent to the Kennedy melee. When both

New York city slickers brought in a ringer

games were over, Kennedy brought his gang over and challenged the high school winners to another go. What's more, he won.

There have been amusing variations on this touchy subject. A group of New York city slickers of the fourth estate once challenged the Washington mob to a game, and appeared with an undersized mite in tow, diffidently asking if it would be all right for him to play. Permission was gleefully granted by the Washingtonians. But on the first play the little fellow intercepted a pass and ran for a touchdown—not at all surprising in view of the fact that he was Eddie Le Baron, a professional football quarterback of note, and the right kind of a ringer to bring along if you're minded to bring one at all. Eddie can hit a gnat in the eye with a running pass at 60 yards distance. But it is indicative of the fitness and drive of the New Frontier team that they bottled him up for the rest of the afternoon on his running plays.

Where did Touch come from?

Basically, of course, Touch is a stepchild of regular football. It is simply football—without crutches. But it goes even further back.

When you follow sports back through the ages, you find an interesting dichotomy, dividing nations into doers and watchers. The Spanish, for instance, an ancient and a cultured race with a history bristling with brave conquest, are not natural sportsmen. But they enjoy the drama and ballet of men and beasts, disputing the right to live with the rite of death.

In contrast, the English are veritable missionaries of participation sports, although perhaps it is not too unexpected that a nation confined to a small and dank island

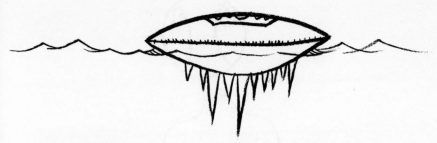

might naturally turn to navigation and sports to expand and keep warm.

It is a relief to note that, for once, although the Chinese and Japanese are there as usual in the lexicons detailing the history of football, that the Egyptians seem to have overlooked it. The Polynesians played it, and so did the Eskimos. Homer mentions football in his Odyssey. And the Greeks had four words for it—*harpaston*, *phenindia*, *episkyres*, and *epikoines*.

It must be remembered that sports in their purest form originated as rehearsals of combat during the boring waiting periods between wars. The incentive was then at its peak. Today an athlete competes for money or glory. In those days, if you were missing an arm or a head, you didn't get to make the trip. So you put your heart into it. We have only ourselves to blame for such modern innovations as good sportsmanship. The Mayan Indians of Yucatan would have none of this hanky-panky. They played a game of Tula, somewhat resembling basketball, in which the idea was to hit a ball through stone rings set into each end of a walled court. It was understood that the captain of the losing team was beheaded immediately. Any regret he may have felt, however, was assuaged by the thought that he

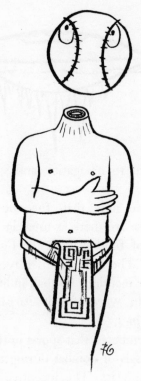

was also a sacrifice in a religious ritual, and thus in a larger sense, the winner.

Sports rules of all sorts were orginally quite simple. Disable your opponent as quickly as possible. Theagenes, the champion pugilist of Greece in 900 B.C., unlike our own fighters who are primarily interested in careers as restaurateurs or real estate operators, killed 1,425 opponents with his fists.

They played football in this spirit. The Spartan warriors lined up any number to a side as long as the totals were even, and attempted by any means to kick or carry

A Roman end and a Celtic quarterback

the ball over the opposite side's goal line. The game often lasted all day, with corpses littering up the field towards evening.

The Romans adopted the game, along with almost everything else, from the Greeks, and called it *follis*. Julius Caesar himself, probably thinking about the conditioning of his legionnaires, considered the game too tame as it was and demanded a revision of the rules.

The Romans carried football with them all over the world. The Celts and the Teutons characteristically preferred to use the skulls of their enemies instead of regulation footballs. The Italians developed a more refined version, called *calcio*, with 27 to a side, including 15 forwards, 5 defensive backs, 4 halfbacks, and 3 fullbacks. The Prince of Mantua, and scions of the House of the Medici, the Rudolfi and the Strozzi, loved the warlike game.

The English, of course, were mad for it. The ruggedness of their foot soldiers through many centuries was due to training on the fields of football. Whole towns played against each other, the only goal being the idea of getting that football—or perhaps a Dane's head dug up from an old battleground—into the other guy's midtown square. Farms were trampled flat, crops and shops destroyed, innocent bystanders dismembered, and in the early fourteenth century, thousands of deaths are chronicled as due to football. Edward II was wroth, not at the butchery, but because "the skill of shooting with arrows was almost totally laid aside for the purpose of football." Richard II, Henry IV, and Henry VIII were also wroth. But they couldn't stop football. Oliver Cromwell himself was a star back at Sussex College, Cambridge.

The game developed in time into a purely kicking

game, as we now know soccer. But the first hero of Touch was lingering in the wings, and in the nineteenth century he made his entrance. There stands on the campus of Rugby College, England, a modest monument with this pleasantly freewheeling inscription:

THIS STONE
COMMEMORATES THE EXPLOIT OF
WILLIAM WEBB ELLIS
WHO WITH A FINE DISREGARD OF THE RULES OF
FOOTBALL, AS PLAYED IN HIS TIME,
FIRST TOOK THE BALL IN HIS ARMS AND RAN WITH IT,
THUS ORIGINATING THE DISTINCTIVE FEATURE OF
THE RUGBY GAME
A.D. 1823

After thus breaking through the ground barrier, Touch suffered a slight setback in the manner of its introduction in this country. Antedating Mr. Ellis, our colonists preferred to foot it lightly without using their hands, and football was actually soccer for nearly a hundred years after the Revolution. The famous game between Princeton and Rutgers in 1869 (which Rutgers won, a habit it has persistently cherished even to this day) is generally recognized as the beginning of intercollegiate football, but it was still just the kicking game. In 1873, Yale, Princeton, Rutgers, and Columbia did their best to form a football league, and of course, Harvard, the daddy of all our colleges, was needed to give the group tone. But up Cambridge way they were playing something called "The Boston Game," which included running with the ball, and Harvard wouldn't join. She even looked to Canada for opponents and played a lively series with McGill University of Montreal, and added to her own version the rugby style brought in by the Canadians. Princeton and Yale then gave the new style a try, and found it good. That settled it—what the Big Three liked, in those days, went. Running with the ball was in.

Subsequently, Harvard invented the flying wedge, and football became a game of massive power against rocklike immovability. Sheer beef was the prerequisite for playing, and the going got pretty rough. An old Blue still tells of the handles sewn on the pants of a light back who was then pitched over the sheer beef. Those were the nose-guard days, although the value of that particular device has always been overestimated, in my opinion. (I once put one on, as a boy—I found the nose guard in an attic at boarding school —and was so impressed with myself that I promptly asked my roommate, a large character, to punch me on the nose

A game of massive power

as hard as he could. He did. He hurt his fist, and granted that my *nose* was unhurt—the guard nevertheless sank so deeply into adjoining areas that for days my eyes felt as if they were popping out, my cheekbones made strange crackling noises, and my sinuses contributed two large purple spots on both sides of my nose. What I needed was a face mask, a device they've produced only recently.)

The beef trust days brought on the dark season of 1905. There were so many deaths and injuries resulting from football in that year that President Theodore Roosevelt threatened to fold up the game if it didn't remove the hazards. The resulting changes in the rules legalized the forward pass.

The pass was not quite home yet, however. The players evidently hated to give up battering each other. Wesleyan, losing to Yale in 1906, threw the very first forward pass, but only one, and then kept right on losing. Yale, unable to score against Harvard, threw a forward pass, and

won the game with it, 6–0. But that was the extent of all
the throwing in all the land.

The pass first came into its own on the wings of those
two football giants, Gus Dorais and Knute Rockne, quarterback and star end of Notre Dame in the 1913 season. Army
had scheduled little Notre Dame that fall as a breather, and
Gus and Knute, working together during the summer at
the same resort, cast around for a way to humble the West
Point juggernaut. They decided on the forward pass, the
forgotten weapon that had been legalized seven years
before and then gone a-begging.

The rest is history, of course. With Gus pitching and
Knute catching, they ran the Army dizzy. And when
the wrathful cadets started booming in on Rockne, Dorais
calmly pitched out to another end, Pliska, who had been
carefully tutored in advance for just such an emergency.
Notre Dame plastered Army 35 to 13. The day of the in-
vincible "big" team was over: the speedy little outfit now
had a chance.

And with the new style of play came Touch. You
don't want to smash your star end to the sod every time
you let him practice catching a pass, so the Tag came in as
a natural substitute for the tackle. Even the heroically pro-
portioned professional footballers today use Touch as part
of their practice repertoire.

The game of football is sheer drama. It has been
abused in recent years and given over to the coaches and
the box office to the extent that undergraduates have been
known to refrain from cheering after a touchdown on the
reasoning that the player was only doing what he was paid
to do. The game is already lost to most of the students as a
participation sport. The coaches are now so open in their

discussions of "recruiting"—a euphemism for purchasing—
that they are outraged only when someone breaks their
unwritten rules and hijacks an athlete already bonded to a
given college, an obvious breach of faith in an already dis-
honorable process.

But the game itself has intrinsic qualities even the au-
thorities cannot destroy, and these it has passed along to
Touch.

Touch is not only The Thing To Do, it is the rewarding thing to do. It offers plenty of body contact for

"... Speed afoot, accuracy and power
in throwing."

those who enjoy the crunch of bone on flesh. It requires
speed afoot, accuracy and power in throwing, skill in catching, stamina in blocking, and strategy in action. It has personal and group appeal. Offense and defense are nicely
balanced. It rewards precision plays as well as inspired
improvisation. It takes you outdoors. Its uniform is the
raggedest outfit in the closet. Somebody usually has an old
football, and if not, a new one is reasonably priced. You
can play, like the Attorney General and his cohorts, anywhere they don't kick you off. You can play to crowds, as

on Staten Island, or you can scamper in the unostentatious privacy of a Bethesda Sunday afternoon.

We need such a game. We need to play it ourselves, in our own communities, as engagingly and enthusiastically as they play it in Washington. We need to teach this game to more growing kids, who are rapidly losing their birthright of participation sports.

The point seems to be that, like the Spanish, we're turning into a nation of watchers.

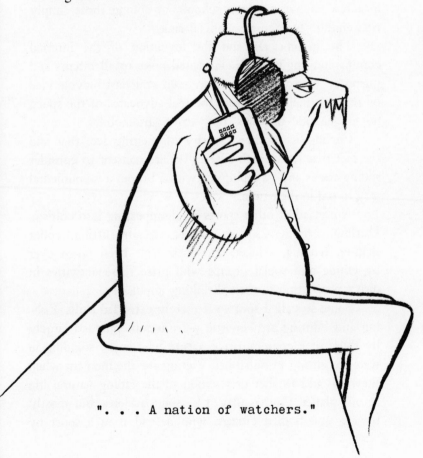

". . . A nation of watchers."

Some of our best sports are already in limbo, the victims of nature or Progress.

Ice hockey and figure skating, for example, are moving ever north with the receding polar line. Linked in with such natural phenomena as the winter traffic in Scandinavian and Russian ports which were traditionally ice-locked in winter or the northern migration of whole breeds of fishes, to the dismay of entire industries, is the fact that ice skaters of any sort will shortly be found only in Canada, in a few of our northern schools, or among those simply rich enough to own an artificial rink.

The income tax and the invention of the internal combustion engine have eliminated polo, to all intents and purposes. And you've probably seen your last bicycle race on this continent. Children, the real advocates of the sport, no longer ride bicycles—they drive automobiles.

Curling is another casualty of melting ice, that and the fact that fewer men every year are content to consider sliding rocks and sweeping ice with a broom a monumental way to put in their time.

A myriad of other sports are disappearing into cultism. Hurling, croquet, squash, soccer, weight lifting, roller skating, fencing, cricket, and chess have been taken over by ethnic and social groups who prize these activities in direct proportion to their shrinking popularity.

Some so-called sports are merely extended skills. Fishing and hunting are atavistic petrifactions pursued largely by those of a contemplative nature who enjoy standing in water or sitting in bulrushes, waiting for the moment when they can add further destruction to the fading natural life of our planet. Golf is played by some athletes, but mostly by less able-bodied citizens who defend it as a sport by

describing the fatigue attendant upon playing eighteen holes—a condition easily duplicated by walking up six flights of stairs and then hanging from a chandelier for ten minutes.

Wrestling is almost exclusively the property of small boys. A few grunters compete in college gyms, to the intense disinterest of their fellows, and the tumblers who perform in public before audiences of senile and juvenile

sadists are undoubtedly something, but they most certainly
are not wrestlers.

Horse racing is a spectacle and a business simply because no one owns a fast horse anymore, except millionaires
and syndicates of near-millionaires.

Track and field records seem to be more dependent
upon the contractors who build the running surface, and
the manufacturers who make devices like vaulting poles,
than upon the athletes themselves.

Automobile racing, a natural product of our mechani-
cal age, is slowly subsiding in its battle against friction, in
the face of space flight at incredible speeds. Crowds still
flock to the races, but they apparently regard the sport
essentially as a jolly way to be in at a killing.

Tennis is natural, but probably not as popular as we
are told. To begin with, its statistics are uncertain. If a
manufacturer sells ten tennis rackets, he reports that there
are ten players, but the chances are that five players bought
an average of two rackets each, which is normal. Public
tennis courts also report great numbers, but a player who
attends three times weekly is listed as three players. And
to top this, court space is diminishing. Country clubs have
their courts, but not as many as they did formerly, and
some have none at all. Tennis clubs are dying off. And all
this is expensive. Playgrounds and rented tennis courts are
victims of the high price of real estate in urban areas. If you
pay six dollars an hour to rent a court, it costs you six cents
every time you tie your shoelace or blow your nose. Tennis
will soon be one with the billiard parlor, the klaxon, and
Billy B. Van's Pine Tree Soap—a nostalgic absentee.

Basketball is currently in the throes of bewilderment at
its own self-destruction. When Dr. Naismith hung up his

peach basket in Springfield, Massachusetts, and contrived
to throw a ball into it for the first time, he devised a game
with marvelous team and virtuoso possibilities. And, indeed,
the skills, stamina, and speed of the professionals and many
of the college players are astonishing. Yet basketball's greatest moment is now in the incongruous stuffing of the ball
through the basket by some beanpole tall enough to look
down on the hoop. At this feat, there is always a great
cheer in the air, made shrill by the fact that most of the
cheerers are youngsters who hope by this vocal magic to
become seven feet tall themselves some day.

The good Dr. Naismith would have wasted no time in
such silly folderol. He would have simply raised the basket
and the standards of the game simultaneously in one sweep-

ing gesture. And, until the lightning strikes, the game will
continue to be a concourse of giraffes, in which six-footers
are looked upon as small men, and those of normal height
as preposterous interlopers.

Baseball has really joined up with the theater and the
circus. It is a kind of an outdoor ballet, in which the rural
beginnings of this country are celebrated by a company of
back-country actors who chew tobacco, have names like
vaudeville performers, and wear boys' pants as they go
about their jobs.

There's something endearing about it, of course, something redolent of one-hoss shays, freckle-faced farm boys
swimmin' in the ole water hole, gossip around the pot-
bellied stove in the general store (that image persists in
the hot-stove league reported every winter in the newspapers) and the small-town hero, knocking one over the
fence with two out in the ninth to make the Fourth of July
celebration perfect for the home folks.

Baseball's whole script is full of this guileless innocence.
The game itself is not the real attraction to the crowds. College baseball players are the loneliest people in the world
—they can hardly induce their own families to sit through a
game as witnesses, much less their fellow students. But the
pros have constructed a never-never land of zany illogic
which sustains itself by a miracle of faith. Managers and
coaches who are hardly literate enough to order a popsicle
are endowed by the crowd with giant intellects and Machia-
vellian cunning, which these mentors express in such gestures of leadership as tugging at their belts, scratching themselves, twiggling their earlobes and noses, as they order
their players to hit-and-run, wait it out, or perform some
other improbables in a game almost wholly controlled by

chance and the vagaries of human error.

The players themselves share the witless charade. They tip their caps a thousand times a game. They spit on their hands. They put dust on their hands. They pound "pockets" into their gloves, already manufactured with the pocket in there. They "talk it up" to a tiring pitcher, as if chatter could restore his waning edge. They hustle. They are the very epitome of the manly virtues invested in The Boy Who Made Good, who saved his money, lived clean, and as a result had a batting average above .300. Meanwhile, the pitchers continue to throw wild to first base, the catchers overthrow second, and the high-priced fielders lose fly balls in the sun while unpaid bleacherites continue to catch anything that comes near them. As often as a manager is fired by his front office for dire incompetence, he is inevitably snapped up by a rival team in a hiring-and-firing farce of musical chairs which rewards failure with a raise.

This is wholly delightful, of course, and no red-blooded American would say a word against baseball. And why should he? Baseball is youth—national youth and the pang of your own boyhood immortalized at least for an afternoon by the crack of bat against ball. It is green grass, and a chance to jostle and shout, and abuse a man in a blue suit, who wears a tiny boy's cap on his head, and carries in his hip pocket the most hilarious symbol of any job in existence, a whisk broom.

It is incredible, zany, financially impressive, and often beautiful to see.

But it is not a sport.

There are not many more sports left to rediscover. Dartmouth has recently taken up rugby with a vim that has dismayed many of their scheduled opponents in Great Britain, but it is a solitary gesture. Lacrosse is an indigenous Indian game, once played by whole communities much as we have seen in football's early days. It was rough-and-ready, and the brave usually put the ball in his mouth in order to use his stick more handily in defending himself from the assaults of his opponents. A thump on the back of the neck was the answer to that particular maneuver, but even such pleasures have not resulted in any widespread enthusiasm for lacrosse. It is played by many colleges, but for some reason the leading teams—including Navy—are all centered in Maryland. So are crab cakes.

It would seem that Touch is our only enduring hope. Let us, therefore, take up the game itself.

Anybody Can Play, Anywhere

IN THE TOUCH FOOTBALL HALL OF FAME, PRESENTLY BEING
RUSHED TO COMPLETION IN SOME PUBLICIST'S IMAGINATION,
perhaps the most treasured photograph is also the most sig-
nificant.

It depicts a group of four, two versus two. No study
of Touch has ever been initiated without a thorough
analysis of this basic photograph. It is to the game what
Brady was to the Civil War.

The action takes place on a beach, recognizable as
the strand at Hyannis Port, Massachusetts. In the fore-

ground, a man is handing off the ball to a woman. In the middle ground, a muscular young man is gathering speed as he rushes in to block the play. In the background, a second male defender stands poised—like the marshal in a Western walkdown, feet apart, arms hooked at sides, fingers outspread at the ready—to handle secondary strategy.

The man handling the ball is Mr. Robert Kennedy, lithe and trim in casual shorts and bare feet. His partner is Mrs. Robert Kennedy, beauteous in a flowered, single-piece swimsuit and sun glasses. The middle-ground defender is Mr. Edward Kennedy, in patterned swim trunks. The determined gent in the background is waiting.

Now the purpose of this examination is not to admire the foursome, although they are obviously admirable. It is to appreciate the depth of meaning here, Touch-wise.

In the first place, Mr. Robert Kennedy has been quoted in a national magazine as stating that "Me and *Ethel* can beat anybody." His partner in this case happens to be Ethel, his wife, the partner with whom he can beat anybody. One may conclude, therefore, that the outcome of this game is a foregone conclusion, though the issue may have appeared in doubt when the picture was snapped.

The entire bearing of this photograph on the history of Touch cannot be overestimated. Note the following points:

1. Mr. Kennedy is in a perfect pose for concealing his intentions from the opposing team. His left shoulder is thrust slightly forward, as he turns to the right for a hand-off to his fair partner. She is running toward him, cutting from the right to the left of the picture, and they have been snapped at the moment of a perfect exchange. Mr.

The Basic Photograph

Kennedy has his right hand under the ball, his left forearm is raised, blocking the view of the handoff from the defense. Mrs. Kennedy, in full flight, has two hands on the ball, and is obviously not going to muff it.

2. Mr. Kennedy has a choice. He may fake the handoff, and run with it himself. He may fake the handoff, fake a run, and throw a pass to Mrs. Kennedy, who will conceivably run around her husband as he closes in on Robert, and thus have to deal with the secondary defense in fielding her pass. Mr. Kennedy may continue with the handoff, run downfield for a pass. Or he may run downfield, drawing the defenders with him—mindful of the fact that he was

once an end for Harvard—and leave Mrs. Kennedy free
for a gainful and doubtless graceful sprint.

3. Mr. Edward Kennedy, of course, realizes all this. The
expression on his face suggests that the alternatives are
futile, since he proposes to get in so fast that the play will
be broken up anyway, by a fast tag.

4. The second defender is in a quandary. He hopes Mr.
Edward Kennedy will break up the play. He has several
reasons for this. One is that Mr. Robert Kennedy is a hell-
for-leather runner and a fine pass receiver, and he takes
Touch seriously. A man like that, coming downfield, is
worth watching closely. The second defender also has
other worries. He may know, for example—since he is
probably a house guest or close political or social ac-

quaintance of the Kennedys—that Mrs. Kennedy is expected to appear at a ball at the Iranian Embassy that night,
perhaps, radiant in a white silk sheath, with off-the-shoul-
der effect. It would not be seemly for her to appear with
the outline of a hand on her shoulder, no matter how re-
spectfully laid on during the game. There are other problems of a similar nature crossing the defender's mind at this
moment which need no further emphasis here. Mr. Fletcher
Knebel, the sage of the Washington scene, offers the opinion that playing Touch with the wives of high-ranking
officials in the Administration is a political pitfall which,
perhaps fortunately for them, Daniel Webster or James
Lansing did not have to face.

5. The picture suggests other interesting facets. Mr. Robert Kennedy is evidently playing with the waters of Nantucket Sound immediately to his right. To his left, the beach
slopes uphill, and a run in that direction would have to be
engineered with this gravity drag in mind. Thus, there is
the chance that he will have to pass or receive a pass on
the Sound side. Hence the pass receiver may well find himself or herself tearing through the edge of the surf. The
equisided stance of the secondary defender makes it very
clear that he considers this one of the possibilities, and by
no means an outside chance. Now, anyone who has run
even casually through the waters of Nantucket Sound
knows that they are rife with clam shells, clumps of sea-
weed, the bones of eroded cuttlefish, discarded whistles
from boxes of Cracker Jack, and waterlogged copies of the
Martha's Vineyard *Gazette*. That is not to say that the
beach at Hyannis Port is littered. Far from it. But even the
most patriotic tides are whimsical.

6. The point is that all the players in this game are bare-

foot. Now, just running in sand is a tiresome exercise. And carried to extreme lengths, hard on the delicate skin between the toes. A couple of fast sprints are usually enough for all but the most conditioned epidermis.. Add to this the possibility of a long goalward dash through the flotsam of Nantucket Sound and you encounter one of Touch's worst obstacles—Toe Fatigue.

7. Students of this classic photograph have occasionally overemphasized the importance of its shadows. Mr. Robert Kennedy, for example, is casting a very long shadow behind him, with the sun originating from the water side. Speculations as to whether it is early morning or late afternoon have no bearing on the subject. But it does look as though he had been the winner of the toss and cannily elected to put the sun in his opponents' eyes.

8. This brief rundown of a typical game of Touch, a mere footnote to studies in depth which have been made of the historic photograph, does have ample bearing, however, on the would-be player who approaches the game in this spirit of this book—i.e., enthusiastically, but warily.

9. Certain inescapable conclusions may be drawn:
   a. Anybody can play.
   b. Anybody can play anywhere.
   c. Anybody can play as long as he wants, contingent on such correlative factors as the sinking (or rising) sun, and the annoyance of running with tiny mollusks between the toes.

10. Therefore, it will be rewarding to take up these groundwork principles in order:

Anybody can play:
   You will note the precise use of the word "can" in the

above heading. It literally means that anybody able to move around *can* play. I am careful not to state that "anybody *may* play." There are those who *can* play and yearn to play, but never *will* play, since Touch has become "the" status game of all time. One of the reasons, of course, is its gay place in the scheme of The New Frontier, as I've noted earlier. Although it is still connected with crab grass, small rocks, patches of dirt, discouraged shrubbery, and ungeometrical topography—as it was when I was an undergraduate—it has also taken on a patina of such 50-dollar words as *élan, éclat, esprit, joie de vivre, wunderkind,* tone, drive, intensity, and other staples in the Kennedy vocabulary. Now, everybody wants these, even at the risk of cutting his big toe on a seashell mollusk (Newspaper item: *he pulled up with a lame mussel*) or falling over a pile of beer cans in Bethesda. So that everybody really wants to play, but only those *may* play who have made the grade. It is a permissive game, in other words. You must belong to The Club. All such clubs are much more closely run than your own country club, for instance, where social pressures are more or less openly applied. This club has nothing to do with race, creed, or condition of bank account. It has subtle and unspoken balances of unspeakably sensitive nuances. During the Eisenhower administration, everyone wanted to be a Good Guy, to create a public image of a man of immense probity, ready to exchange a joke or a slap on the back with any other similar human being, and smiling broadly at all times to prove that any errors might be due to inability, perhaps, but never to any desire less than doing The Right Thing. The New Frontier has its own brand of insistent integrity, but it is concerned less with an image of crowd-pleasing popularity

than an image of crowd-moving leadership. These look just like words at first—but they are not, really. The slight turn of the political dial was all that was necessary to make golf an Out game, and Touch an In game.

That is not to say that Touch, outside of Washington, has become any less subtle in its group symbolism. In the smallest hamlet in the nation, the broadest smile and the heartiest slap on the back—unless it is an out-and-out Tag —will get you nowhere in Touch, but hustle and drive will. You get with it in Touch, with all you've got. Otherwise, you're turned back into the outer reaches where dwell those who *can* play, but *may* not.

Among those who may play, of course the Touchiest subject is *les girls*.

We have to except, with deep regret, all the Kennedy

girls. They are charming, vivacious, and ladylike, to the last of them, and since they *are* Kennedy girls, it follows— *voilà*—that they play Touch. But they play on Olympic strata like the White House lawn, and so are above comment.

But the Kennedy girls have set a national pattern. Girls everywhere want to play Touch, and no *may* about it. So it is sensible to anticipate what you'll be up against as the chief proponent of Touch in your neighborhood.

The first type you'll be apt to run up against is The Ivy Girl. Broadly defined, she is one of the lassies who attend Barnard, Cornell, Pembroke, Radcliffe, and the College for Liberal Arts at the University of Pennsylvania, and thus by actual membership (tied with Columbia, Cornell, Brown, Harvard, and the University of Pennsylvania, by official decree) are in the League. There are also those who are in the League via invitation, rather than matriculation, which is where Dartmouth, Yale, and Princeton put in their Ivy votes. These fair wayfarers spring from Smith, Wellesley, Vassar, Mount Holyoke, Bryn Mawr, Skidmore, Bennington, Sarah Lawrence, Sweetbriar, and other such leafy outposts, with plenty of vigah for the Ivy tradition.

The Ivy girl has cultivated her own special kind of allure, firm in the belief that companionability is the key to daytime popularity, and that at night nature will take over for her, since it both can and may. There is nothing coy or flirtatious about her. She has been unconsciously schooled—at home and in her training and "finishing"— in the art of getting along "famously" with men. She scorns the girlish vocabulary and point of view favored by working girls or college groups elsewhere in the country. She has cultivated attitudes, speech, and even tones of voice that

are gentle editions of the male Ivy Leaguer's. Her posture
is carefully unfeminine. She does everything possible to
avoid the seductive or the suggestive. She does not have
silly hair-dos, but goes either beatnik or boyish, leaving the
Italian and French bird's-nest fads to the less secure working girl. She walks like her Ivy League date, slouching and
pointing her toes out. Her voice is a flat monotone—shrieks
and feminine squeals are out. She speaks in brief, quiet
understatement. (Later, when she joins the Junior League,
her voice may sink to a baritone, and she will speak in brief,
quiet overstatement, but that is another book altogether.)

This Ivy girl takes Touch as a matter of course. On
any Ivy campus on a Saturday or Sunday morning in the
golden autumn, you'll find her playing Touch with the
boys behind the House, or in front of the Dorm, in a proper
corollary to the Big Game played that weekend in the
Stadium, which no one in the League takes very seriously
anymore, except the coach and some of the more determined
squares among the alumni.

She plays a good game, too. She's agile, tougher than
you might expect from what is currently defined as a "soft
boy," and she's smart in devising and carrying out trick
plays.

With the Ivy girl, your danger is not on the field. She
won't break into tears if she falls down. She'll make her
share of the Tags. She'll even throw a surprise pass or two.
Rate her at about 45 percent of your own ability and you'll
be able to plan the correct strategy in depth—she can throw
a straight pass but not a long one.

Your danger comes later. Ivy League girls never expect praise if they make a touchdown. They expect affection, after the game. This may be your idea of scoring or

The Ivy Girl

not—I'm just pointing out the probabilities.

The second most frequent danger in the field is one I must ungallantly call The Hammerthrower. I do not especially want to suggest by this that our outstanding girl athletes have any connection with the considerable numbers of Olympic members of European teams who habitually take out official papers as members of the Male Sex after the Games have concluded. But in this country, a sympathetic male must realize that the girls are up against it. Having convened at Seneca Falls in the latter part of the nineteenth century, adopted that hideous bifurcated garment subsequently dubbed bloomers after their creator, and determined that the only way to invade the realms of male privilege was to become his equal in every endeavor, they also made the mistake of including physical effort in that Bill of Rights.

We know today the ghastly effects of that decision. Women have the vote and they have electrical appliances, but they are failing as executives as well as wives. And certainly they are preposterous in most forms of physical endeavor, except possibly swimming and certain forms of gymnastics involving grace and fluid strength.

In Touch, therefore, beware The Hammerthrower. The poor girl is the extreme sample of the equality psychosis of the species. Most probably she is an ex-Captain of Field Hockey from a woman's college. At coed universities, girls rarely try to excel in athletics. They like to beat the boys at debating or writing theses in Greek, and—somewhat to their own surprise—they make damn good scientists. But they lay off the leadership bit that means so much in the women's colleges. They're aware, for example, that in a coed school, the best a girl can hope for is the vice-presidency of her class—a man always gets the No. 1 job. But in the women's colleges, she can make it to The Top, in athletics as well as campus politics. Hence, she enjoys a sense of power at an early age. And, beware of running into this dame in Touch. The frumious bandersnatch is no more to

The Hammerthrower

be dreaded. The ex-field-hockey champ is out to make you miserable simply because you are a man, whether you're on her team or not. If she's opposing you, keep away from her. She'd like to ground you as often as possible (and she takes the idea literally). If she's on your side, she'll stay there for a while, but after a bit you'll begin to discover that she's really on quite another team, known as The Women. And her job is to make you, a man, look bad as often as possible.

In addition, she does not expect affection after the game. She expects another game as soon as possible, in recognition of her prowess, and it may consist of tennis, drinking, discussing Kafka, or hand wrestling.

Avoid all this by refusing to let her into the game. Tell her the sides are already chosen, especially if you've already got a girl in the lineup. If not, tell her that Touch is only for men. This will only confirm her suspicions about you, that you are a latent homosexual, and out to prove your maleness. So you just grin, walk away, and bear it. After all, latent isn't so bad.

Your other cross may be the girl-type girl, or poor-little-me character. She habitually uses the coaching attitudes of golf, tennis, swimming, and diving, as a chance to suggest that she really is a better athlete than you divine, but that she'd like to enjoy a little delicious dalliance with a godlike muscularity like yourself before getting into the prosaic stretches of the sport itself.

Don't let her kid you. She feels great, to the touch, but for Touch, she's awful. Make with a little dalliance, if you have the time. Show her how to pass. Throw a few blocks at her. Then, forgetting the game entirely, ask her what she's doing after the scrimmage. That's what she had on her mind in the first place. And if your play chart is clear in your own mind, there'll be only token opposition ahead.

More often, however, you'll be picking male players, and there's more reason involved here, and less evasion. Girls you want to avoid, men you want to play.

But like anyone setting out on a career, one must approach Touch with the utmost realism. Let us recognize from the beginning that you are not doing this wholly for the exercise. Otherwise you would be working out in a gym, or if you needed the air, doing the same things outdoors. No—Touch has important social and personal overtones which must be faced unflinchingly. And they are of supreme importance, *before* the game.

If you are to be just a player, pass a friendly word or two with the captain you prefer, either just before the game, or maybe a day before the game. Let him know you'd consider it a privilege to be on his side.

Now, if he's high in the Federal Government, he *knows* it's a privilege to be on his side. Your innuendo then must suggest that it's a pleasure just joining up with such a jolly specimen of the human race.

Whatever you do, forget about who's going to win until the game starts. Get on the side with the most influential captain. If you can't make it, then play like hell against him, and make *him* want *you*.

Similarly, if you are picking players, start out by forgetting their abilities. All things considered, it is better to have a thoroughly winded and somewhat spavined Head of a Department on your side than the most agile and well-conditioned junior aspirant from a lower echelon. This applies in village Touch as well as in Washington, D.C., and is known as Scaling the Possibilities.

After you've adjusted your sights to the political and economic realities, carefully sounding out Avagadro's Hypothesis (I refer not to the nineteenth century physics man but to Tony Avagadro, who is a bartender at the Chevy Chase Club, in Maryland, just outside of the capital) that you can rate a player by dividing his bank account by his point potential, and then dividing this figure by 100. Thus, if Habbakuk Agememnon, recently appointed to the Judiciary, has a cool million in cash in the bank, and still looks fit enough to score ten points, you divide the million by ten, and the resulting hundred thousand by one hundred. That leaves Habbakuk shaping up as a 100 percent possibility, a good man to have on your side in any league.

Avagadro's Hypothesis is applied with equal ease to potential players whose value may be scaled in terms of publicity or propaganda. For example, if Cecil Trenchmouth and Gormley Hardscrabble III are equally penurious, but represent the Sapling Fence Association and *Life* magazine respectively, the Avagadrian slide rule immediately awards Trenchmouth a theoretical bank balance of $10,000 and Hardscrabble about $2,500,000. Applying the Hypothesis, then, to these corrected figures one reaches a rating figure of 10 for Cecil and 2,500 for Gormley.

The alert captain will make his selections accordingly.

Touch, you begin to realize, has a Grand Design to it, as well as a swagger air.

But there is a smaller pattern involved in the selection of players not to be overlooked by the alert captain.

That concerns actual abilities on the field, after the Hypothesis has been applied.

These are not always what they may seem. We have

already learned that although Touch may be played by the young, it is not exclusively their province. Psychological factors involve performance and results almost as much as do physical factors.

For example, one would ordinarily think that ex-football stars would be prime Touch players. In one respect they are—it is almost imperative that they outdo the next fellow for the sake of pride, even despite protesting twinges in the left ventricle of the heart. But in most other ways, they're a bad risk. They talk a terrific game, interlarding references to the present scrimmage with reminiscences of past triumphs, trailing clouds of glory as they come. Similarly, old varsity men are usually beer drinkers, and take on more cargo as the game progresses. A good Scotch man can usually run rings around them, if he can run at all.

Look closely at the fingers of each player. Pick the ones who are badly stained with nicotine. Steady smokers play a relaxed game. Nonsmokers press too hard.

Pick a man with a beard immediately. Living up to a beard is worth six points to any team before the game starts.

A couple of large, out-of-condition hulks will be useful, even if you suspect they have flattened their feet by their own weight. This type runs out of gas after a few plays, and is seemingly useless. Not so, however. They become practically immobile, and may be used as stationary obstacles for standing block plays. They are immovable as well as immobile, since they *can't* be moved aside even if the opposition tries to shove them out of there. A canny captain will realize that a couple of these behemoths are at least as valuable as one tree and a stump in planning his attack.

As a final word in selecting players, avoid by all means

"Don't ever play with your boss!"

those who look at you with keen and alert eyes, who walk with a spring in their step, and who move with a quickness suggesting speed on the field. This is all a sham put on for your benefit. The real athletes have no need for this camouflage and may be found slouching around and smoking, or leaning wearily on each other comparing hangovers. These are your boys. Once the game starts, they'll run like the wind to overcome their natural lethargies.

The natural wisdom of being a player, and among those selected, is also a touchy subject. Your choice should be clear: when to play and when not to play.

Gentlemen who have reached the retirement age without having to make discreet inquiries at the poorhouse beforehand, are agreed that Touch invites certain propinquities which involve the pursuit of happiness more closely than those of the ball-carrier. Their warnings are crystalline, and bell-like in clarity:

1. *Don't ever play with your boss.*

At first blush, an employee is usually happy and excited by the idea of social contact with his employer. It seems, he calculates, the ideal atmosphere in which to unveil certain sterling virtues which office procedure keeps under wraps, such as brilliant strategy, stamina, joy of living, companionability, *noblesse oblige, mens sana in corpore sano*, and all that old-school-tie kind of thing.

I warn you against this with the same solemnity with which I would adjure you to refrain from wearing a bee beard. The newsreels used to be, and the newspapers occasionally are in a time of drought, populated by photographs of men standing in front of a hive, with a beard of friendly bees, the little insects having deserted their waxworks to serve as a chin covering, each holding on to the hind legs of the worker in front of them. I have often wondered why these men have never gone in for something more stylish, like, say, a mustache of yellow jackets, or a wasp toupee. But we'll let that go for the moment. And let the bees go, too. Leave them to apiarists in New Zealand who climb Mt. Everest.

My bee image is deliberate in that the pain potential when playing Touch with your boss is far more serious than merely winding up with a lumpy face. The reason is that he doesn't see you the way you see him. One of the great American misconceptions is that the top executive of any sizable firm is an intellectual giant with a head teeming with facts and figures, ideas, and a comprehensive grasp of industry, society, and government. The fact is much more likely that he seized on the truth early in life that brains and talent may be easily purchased and then quickly got himself up on the levels where these things are bought. The executive psyche is sinewy and simplified; it is concerned with directions rather than details. Therefore, although it may be incomprehensible to you, the executive mind is quite capable of relating that raise you were hoping for with the forward pass you just dropped, or the honesty of your expense account with your claim that you tagged him before he reached the goal line. If you play well, it may occur to him that you are more interested in weekend sports than in company problems. If you play poorly, he may sense in you a hitherto unsuspected lack of dedication.

Skip it. If anyone mentions Touch, and your boss hasn't moved over to the bar, go there yourself. What's more, if there's a chance in the world that he will recognize you, hide behind it.

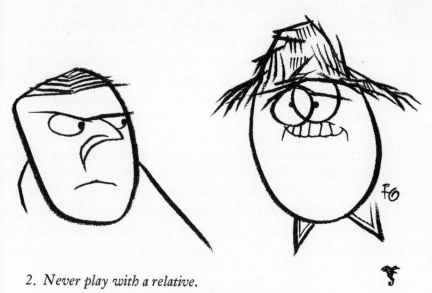

2. *Never play with a relative.*

This applies both to blood relations and in-laws, regardless of the tribal inclinations of the Kennedys. The pecking order, which is the natural foundation of any true family group, is never in better working shape than on the field of Touch. Your older brothers and your uncles, feckless incompetents though they may be at the game, will inevitably confuse chronological status with captaincy rights, and bad blood will result no matter how pure your family strain. If you play with your in-laws, it will be immediately revealed to you that your wife has somehow sprung from a strain badly infiltrated with the Jukeses and the Kallikaks, and that her little lovable weaknesses of character you have been so nobly putting up with are really the result of inbreeding among a company of swineherds and basket weavers.

3. Never play with occupational associates.

The hazard is obvious. After all, you do need the regard of your fellow workers. Let's say that you are a comb dentist, professionally: that is, your job is to spot-check the teeth of pocket combs in a plastic factory, determining the balance factor of fine teeth at one end of the comb versus the broad teeth at the other. If you put up a bad show on the field, your fellows in the shop will inevitably relate this to cavities in the assembly line, and to the plummeting sales chart of All-Fines, the comb you predicted was The Coming Thing. If you shine on the field, the fellows will put you down as a show-off, one who is apt to be passed by when the plant diversifies in the modern trend, takes on hair brushes, and needs able men for the bristle shop.

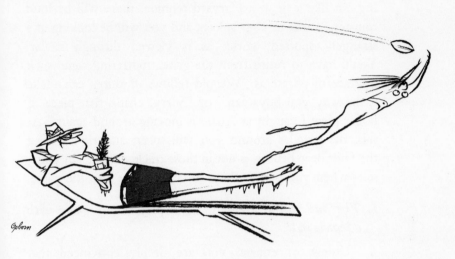

4. Consider the size and age of the group.

Big men, when aroused, are more trouble to handle than little men. Therefore, if it looks as though you're going to spend the afternoon ineffectually trying to claw your way up some six-footer's back in order to intercept a pass, or propose to have your chest cavity ringing like a drum every time that Old Blue gives you a standing block with a tattoo of elbows on your ribs, you'd better fade. Similarly, watch out for youths who make a career out of being young, especially track men. If you've ever watched a runner jog around before a race, loosening up, and then jog around after a desperately run two-mile, cooling out, you'll know what I mean. Any sensible man would rest before and after the race, saving his energies and trying to figure out a way to avoid running at all. But these boys fashion a career out of making the walk obsolete. Keep away from this type. In fifteen minutes you'll have your tongue hang-

ing out like a tie at a Harvard reunion, there will be loud
tom-tom noises in your spleen, and you will be looking at a
strangely spotted world, as if viewed through caviar.
You'll have to retire from the game, muttering some such
disgraceful phrase as "We old fellows of thirty can't take
it the way you boys can," or "Sorry, chaps, that piece of
boiler plate I caught at Anzio is moving around again." At
this, the gazelles around you will sneer, and rightly. But
the fault dear Brutus, is not in those track stars. It's in yourself—when you permit them to chivvy you into the game.

5. *The final rule is needless. Don't play in any game with
a female in it.*

Unless, of course, you are deeply convinced that
women never use tears as a weapon, are innately good
sports, will live up to the rules implicitly, and will not inter-
pret your running, passing, and tagging techniques as per-
verse sexual manifestations.

Now, if you find that none of these exceptions above
are in force, and you really do want to play, there are several effective gambits you can use.

1. *That old feeling.*

You don't say anything. You just reach down, being
careful to stand somewhere near the captain, pick up the
football and heft it a little. Smile wistfully, and shake your
head in a kind of puzzled affection—as though someone
mentioned the name of a wonderful old girl friend of yours
you've been missing lately. Then, take the ball in your
passing hand and bang it into the palm of your other hand.
Don't just push it or toss it. Bang it. As it makes a loud,

slamming noise in your palm, you nod. Do it a couple of times. Bang, nod. Bang, nod. Bang, nod. Then you look up and catch your would-be captain's eye. The message is obvious: you've found out that the ball is the right kind, no kid stuff here, and you're willing to let a real pro—yourself—mix in with the amateurs, now that you know the equipment is up to par. As your eyes meet his, you nod slightly again. The nod says: *"Let's go, old buddy. Never mind the rest of these clowns. You and I can take them alone, just the two of us."*

2. *The strategy bait.*

This is also man-to-man stuff, but verbal. In the quiet, assured tones of one accustomed to being heard, even in the babble of underlings, you inquire of the captain: "Any rules against overshifting or red-dogging?" If he dismisses you on this, give him another: "Are we geared for the banana-and-go or the buttonhook-and-go?" This'll shake

him, unless he's already read the first part of this chapter and looked into your bank account.

3. *The rapid vapid.*

You couldn't care less. You sit on a stump, or lie on the ground, eyes closed, at peace with the world. The implication: you're your own man, whatever the choose-up, and whoever picks you is going to be on the high-scoring side. If you want to underscore this, and you happen to be wearing a long-sleeved shirt, roll up the sleeve of your throwing arm *but not the other one.* The suggestion here is that you're going to be throwing plenty of long, straight ones that afternoon, and the sooner the better.

4. *The badge.*

Wear something official-looking. It can be as innocent as a knee brace or a wrist strap, but it must suggest that you are accustomed to hard-nosed exercise and revel in it. You will, of course, beware of anything as ostentatious or déclassé as a sweater with your varsity letter or class numerals on it. But a pair of old trunks, obviously left over from a basketball *uniform*—perhaps in color with piping along the sides—a squad jacket cast carelessly on the grass or a pair of heavy wool socks in stripings or coloration reminiscent of baseball or football team equipment, all will do wonders.

Let us assume, that you are ready to play.

The sides have been chosen purely on a pick-up basis, a gathering of kindred spirits brought together by a common interest in exercise *per se.*

On one side are Krishna Menon, Truman Capote, Brigitte Bardot, the Archbishop of Canterbury, Roger

Blough, and Martin Chuzzlewit, a character out of Dickens, Iowa.

On the other are the six Debonnaires, a glockenspiel combo which renders its numbers while riding unicycles, and enjoys a vociferous following in the Maritime Provinces.

The die is cast; the lists are entered; the field is taken.

Anybody Can Play, Anywhere

The decision as to where to play is almost wholly up to chance and geography. In Tiffany's, conceivably, they play in the main aisle, tossing a natural pearl as big as a football for touchdowns 'way down by the elevators, which are used to keep score by being driven to various floors as the numbers mount up.

In my own youth, we played in the Cathedral Close where I was a choirboy. The older boys favored a lawn over by the Bishop's House where certain interesting views of happenings in the nearby hospital for women might be occasionally offered to the farsighted. Smaller sportsmen kept to the lawns, however, and on a lawn run were compelled to zigzag among monolithic chunks of marble and granite awaiting fixment in the unfinished structure of the Cathedral. One false step in that maze of hard-rock obstacles and you had a barked shin or scrape along the side of the scalp which would leave you tingling for life—as I am—at the sound of the word "Touch."

In later years I attended a day school which worked out in New York City's Central Park. Of this park it may be said, and even more so today, that there are inevitably four or possibly six teams available for every Touch field. Since they all arrived firmly intending to play, and commenced on the nearest field the minute the occupying teams swirled into another area of the field, the result was an interlocking maelstrom of passes and curses. There were parochial hazards such as nannies with their prams, old men sunning themselves on benches or on slablike rocks, angry city dogs who are beyond all canine psychiatry, and patrols of fleet-footed little boys who laid in wait for a wandering ball, and made off with it to parts unknown at an incredible speed. We used to have to post one of our fastest runners purely as a guard and pursuit officer.

The three games on the one field were the most puzzling hazard, of course. A young man in the Midwest has recently invented a game of three-dimensional chess which exploits all the well known mathematical variants within the classic game to an astronomical conjecture. Our game of Touch was somewhat the same. Apparently in the clear for a pass, you found yourself either rubbed out by a charging line of Bessarabian sausage-makers (locked in mortal combat with the team from Slaughterhouse #14, owned by Sol Meyers of Throg's Neck, the Bronx, who donated the cup) or the pass was snatched from your hands by a healthy and heavy-breathing Amazon from St. Agatha's School for Girls, hard by the Park. It was a fine outing, and on one occasion reached a glorious peak which made all other exertions superfluous forever—I caught two passes on one run. Our claim for two touchdowns was disallowed but, as I recall, the foreign ball which floated into our milieu and

was thus carried over the goal line—according to its owners
—was thus worth six points to *them*, having hit pay dirt
by whatever means.

The temptation here is not to write an autobiography,
but, in an excess of modesty, to skip the one full-fledged
case history available to us without applying thumbscrews
or the Iron Maiden to my friends. It is essential for those
about to Touch to understand the uses of improvisation in
the selection of a field.

My own subsequent wanderings for Touch involve
two experiences that underline the ultimate moral of this
book in your hand. In my college days, a regular series of
Touch was played out on the spacious campus. There were
also about thirty thousand square miles of meadows in the
adjacent countryside, but we naturally turned to the sparse
real estate of our own fraternity house. High-minded edu-
cators who hope for the immediate demise of the fraternity
system have on their side the most effective allies of all—
the filthy furniture and inept housekeeping of these domi-
ciles, the inferior food, and the necessity to nourish grounds
and landscaping that obviously don't deserve it. Our own
method, common to all fratenity houses, was to use what
ground was available as an athletic field. This brought up a
number of particular problems. Even students of today will
recognize the genre—at Wisconsin, a man running for a
pass may find himself in Lake Mendota; at Cornell he may
wind up in Cascadilla Gorge or in a cow barn; only, it
would seem, at Yale with its architecturally stern quad-
rangles—rectangles of grass creating an inner court sur-
rounded by the buildings of each "College"—is the course
ideal for Touch. We had none of this. Our field was behind
the House: it was bounded on one side by a stone wall, on

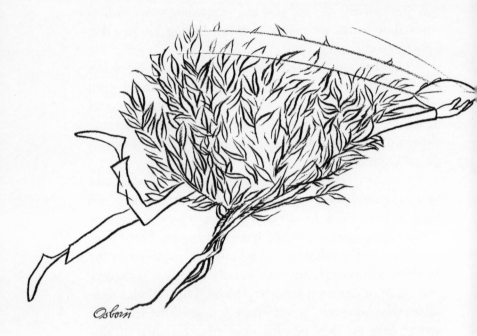

Osborn

the opposite by the discouraged building shrubbery and
an open flight of cellar stairs. At one end of the field it im-
pinged on the grounds of the next fraternity house (and the
inevitable game in progress there), and on the other, since
our House was a corner plot, the Touch field was bounded
by a sidewalk. We were across the street from the area hospital, and as a result we were probably the only Touch ag-
gregation before or since which utilized as one goal line a
stream of nurses. The angels of mercy left the hospital and
walked along the sidewalk to their own dormitory, which
was our neighbor of the odd-corner side. The girls made a
very satisfactory white target for touchdown passes. Of
course, they scattered like doves as the players descended
on them, and frequently suffered minor injuries in the

fracas, but they were the best goal posts on record. To balance this ineffable good luck, the stone wall and the cellar stairs were adequately threatening. Shrubbery on any Touch field is at best a nuisance. A lilac bush, run into at full tilt, protests, but supports at the final moment of impact. Barberry reaches out to trip and scratch, but unless you're bare-legged, you'll survive. A dry wall, however, made up of rocks with a large percentage of granite,

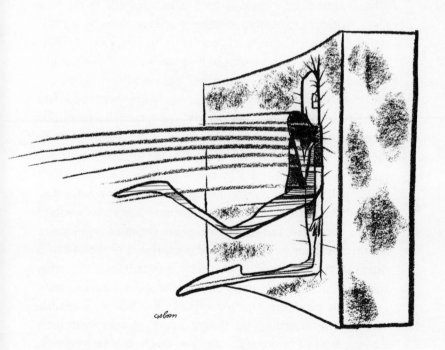

capable of surviving glaciers and therefore scornful of mere
flesh and bone, is another kind of hazard indeed. Even then,
ends on our team preferred that direction by far to the maw
of the cellar stair. The steps could be negotiated by anyone
not too stuffily concerned over breaking legs, arms, or
back (after all, the hospital was mighty handy) but the
main menace was what Gus, our defeated janitor and
guardian of three of the other Houses, might leave on the
steps in the way of rakes, cutting shears, barrels, or parts of
stoves and automobiles he collected at regular trips to the
town dump. A man flailing around those steps with a broken
arm might possibly poke out an eye or lose an ear in the
pincers of one of Gus' old pieces of rusty ironwork, and
what is worse, miss the pass he was running for in the first
place. Characteristically, nothing was ever done about the
stairway, either to cover it, or to tell Gus to quit embellish-
ing it. It remained as an official in-bounds, and if you caught
the pass down there in that cave, and could then negotiate
the stair without being tagged, you were permitted full
freedom of flight. Needless to say, the quarterbacks of our
teams relied heavily on this rule—they'd run a play close to
the stair about every third time, and then instruct one
player to secrete himself in the well after the play. With
good luck, he'd be overlooked and in the clear for a fast
pass on the next play. This strategy was particularly effective in the early fall when the game included sophomore
brothers unfamiliar with the premises. But it proved to be a
disadvantage in the long run—our quarterbacks, directing
the team in official games out on the main campus, were
lacking in plays due to their loss of their stairwell gambit,
and also suffered in their judgment of distance without a
moving wall of white-clad nurses to mark scoring territory,

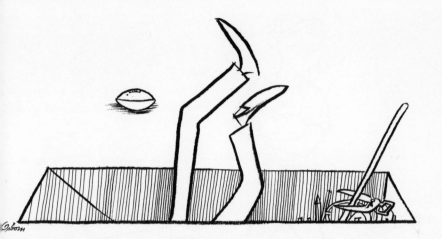

so we usually offered a ragbag kind of game.

Our moment of truth came on another field, close by, where many of the students worked as dishwashers and waiters in an eating club. The club also fed a prep school student group, and the building was next to the school playing fields. It was natural, therefore, in the lulls during our work, when the paying guests were chomping on the food, for the dishwashing crew (of which I was captain) to get up a Touch team (of which I became quarterback in the inevitable interplay of social economics which the game seems to engender).

Thus, since most of the dishwashers were from the same fraternity, we discovered one of the basic principles of Touch, so precisely followed by the Attorney General himself. It is: always play on the other fellow's field, since it is usually better.

In our case, we traded in a cramped and positively dangerous scraggle of grass behind the House, for a well

turfed football field kept up by a strong-spirited and well-
to-do prep school. Our status as college students gave us
the moral stature to accomplish what was in effect a theft
in occupancy; the benign faculty of the prep school, eager
to place its graduates among our number in the college
every year, looked the other way as we enjoyed their
premises.

That is the primary rule which should govern the lo-
cation of your own Sunday games of Touch. Your first target should always be a school. If you fail there, of course a
public playground will do. But schools have a way of so
nauseating their attendants by their conformity of appear-

ance, by their educational rigors, and even by their odor,
that on Sundays they are the most deserted real estate in any
community, including even the station parking lot. Which
brings up another strong possibility—as everyone knows, no
suburban high school boy will consent to attend classes
without a car to drive thereto, even if he lives only a block
away. It isn't really, in my belief, that he is physically lazy
or incapable of the muscular effort; it is simply that he
recognizes that, without a car, his love life will be thwarted,
his friends nonexistent, and the faculty will quite reasonably
suspect him as the perpetrator of the numerous petty thefts
which go on constantly in every well run school. During
weekdays, a private check on the high school parking lot
in my own community revealed, for instance, no less than
five Mercedes-Benz automobiles, four Jaguars, two Cadil-
lacs, the usual motorized army of MG's, and slightly out-
of-date but extremely well kept Buick, Ford, Chevy, Olds-
mobile, and Chrysler convertibles. There were no jalopies.
There was one bicycle, belonging to the principal. So it

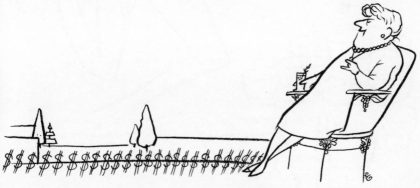

". . . A lawn is not 'grass'--it is an
investment."

Boobytraps!

happens that in most of our communities, while land may come at prices up to $10,000 for a plot, and the grade school may be badly in need of a lunchroom, better plumbing facilities, or even books, that a major municipal appropriation is for the high school parking lot.

On Sunday, however, the brave parade of automotive hardware is miraculously absent. So, if you wish, here is a macadam strip ready for your game of Touch. It is harder on the feet than grass, but you'll slip less. And it is usually already lined, in the hieroglyphics of the parking design, uniform enough to use as markers for the conformation of the field you want.

Before leaving the Field, however, and going on to the Play, we should consider a few *don't's*.

The main prohibitions are against certain temptations that may lead you into social disaster. It should be—but apparently isn't—clear to everyone that athletic prowess, unless barely hinted at, is a better means of getting yourself thoroughly disliked in the social sense than any other talent, except possibly singing. The lad who feels that he is impressing everyone with the beauty and grace of his swan dives is probably catching the eye of very few girls, who are more apt to be lolling in the shade and drinking with less muscular but more amusing types. Furthermore, he is probably stirring up waves that prevent Mrs. Wildershot III, the host's rich aunt and his only hope for retirement above the peon level, from teaching her third-born to swim down at the shallow end of the pool.

In the same sense, don't be the leading spirit in getting up a jolly game of Touch on your host's lawn. Guests are apt to consider lawns as ideal locations for games of catch, badminton, wrestling, or turning backflips terminating with the loud thud of heels digging into the turf. There's an old British saying that to make a good lawn, you turn under the best grass seed you can buy, and then wait five hundred years. All hosts know this to be untrue, because they've tried it. It takes a thousand years, and, after that, the services of a contractor to do it right. As a result, to a host a lawn is not "grass"—it is an investment. You'll do better to walk on the toes of your hostess than on her grass, if it comes to a choice, and she'll be thankful to you besides.

In addition, lawns are flanked by booby traps in the form of beds of prize posies, coy statuary, flowerpots, garden hoses with shaky attachments to shakier outside faucets, sleeping pet cats, and wheelbarrows—all lying in wait to brand you the perfect boob and favorite uninvited guest—and there is always the moment when you stretch for the glorious catch just as the tray of Martinis is borne onto the scene. He who falls with his own Martini is doomed forever, but he who destroys the Martinis of others is consigned to an outer space where the pouring of hot lead down the throat, or flicking out of eyeballs with hors d'oeuvre forks is regarded as pleasant preliminaries to the main chastisement.

You may be just as unhappy if you follow in the footsteps of an overenthused host. Wild horses could not draw from me any derogatory comments anent Miss Elsa Maxwell, whose social triumphs I follow avidly. But I recall that at one time she bade the guests at some high-toned Riviera party dance in an empty swimming pool. I'm sure they loved it. But if Elsa or anyone else tries to shoo you into an empty swimming pool for Touch, cease and desist, as well as resist, immediately. The playing surface will be full of plant life, uneven, and furthermore, your hostess

Bad pass!

might get the idea of turning on the water in the middle of the game and converting it to water polo, a form of damp suicide fit only for grampuses.

In my own present reincarnation of Touch, we play on a country field which was originally designed to hold about five thousand celebrants, gathered together for folk dancing, political rallies, or other forms of riot. The field is adequate—about a half mile long by four hundred yards wide. The possibilities are infinite: it is bounded by a stream, a railroad, a highway, a deep stand of trees, a smattering of comfort stations, a bandstand, and it is also used as a weekend garage for steam rollers, dredgers, stone crushers, and other mammoth impedimenta which assist the gigantic field itself in reducing the players to the stature of darting pygmies. Playing here is more than an exercise, it is a religious experience comprehended only after a lifetime devoted to the study of comparative theologies, centering around a vertical dedication to Zen. A touchdown in this atmosphere, therefore, takes on the same significance as a thunderstorm, the left mandible of a beetle, a drop of dew, or the heavy eyebrows of Uncle Zacharias, the only bachelor in your family, who naturally adores children. It is a place of movement, and of stillness, therefore, definite as well as indeterminate. Perfect for Touch, in other words.

Having thus plumbed the heights as well as the depths of the world of Touch, one draws a deep breath and turns to the end in view—play.

The whistle blows: we now know what to do. We must examine next how to do it.

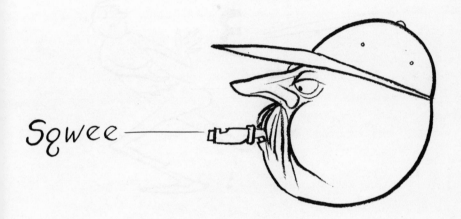

Sqwee

Touch and Go –
The Play's the Thing

IN EXPLAINING HOW TO PLAY THE VARIOUS POSITIONS ON A
TOUCH FOOTBALL TEAM, I AM GOING TO PERSONALIZE IT IN
terms of the two pickup teams which gathered together
down on the school field just a few paragraphs back.

Let us fix them in your mind in their proper positions.
Here is the way they will line up:

(THE SIX DEBONNAIRES)

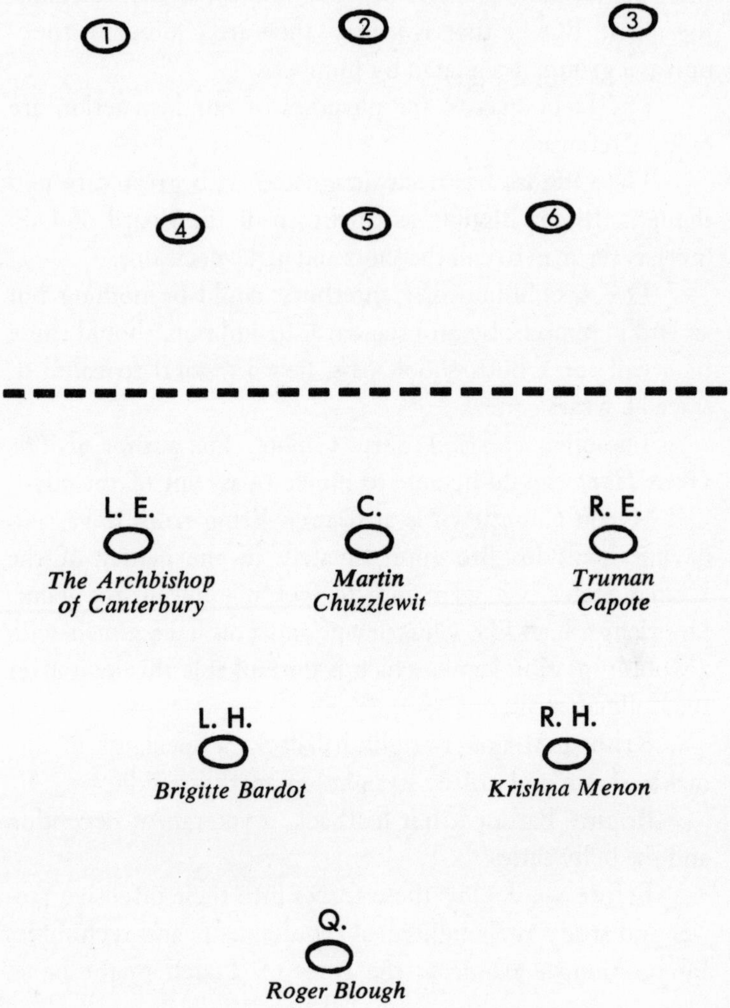

①   ②   ③

④   ⑤   ⑥

- -

L. E.
○
*The Archbishop
of Canterbury*

C.
○
*Martin
Chuzzlewit*

R. E.
○
*Truman
Capote*

L. H.
○
Brigitte Bardot

R. H.
○
Krishna Menon

Q.
○
Roger Blough

The six Debonnaires have stacked their unicycles against a tree and take to the field with the same anonymity they display in their musical combo—they play as a team, there are no stars, possibly because no one has any outstanding talent. But be that as it may, they are content to function as a group, designated by numbers.

The Debonnaires, for purposes of our instruction are on the Defense.

The Offense has been designated with great care and thought. Roger Blough, as Chairman of the Board of U.S. Steel, is the man to call the shots and make decisions.

The Archbishop of Canterbury could be nothing but an end in himself, by any standard. In addition, should there be a call for a buttonhook pass, he's a natural to catch it, since he wears gaiters.

The other end is Truman Capote. The author of *The Grass Harp* should be able to pluck a pass out of the air.

Martin Chuzzlewit is at Center. Being from Iowa, and having spent his life approximately in the center of the United States, we want him to feel at home in the game. Disorient a man like Chuzzlewit, and you have a man with a wobbly passing game, which is unthinkable this long after the Pullman strike.

Krishna Menon is right halfback, a specialist in off-tackle slants and passes straight down the middle.

Brigitte Bardot is left halfback, a veteran of deception and the belly series.

Before we deploy these forces into their offensive tactics and study their individual requirements and techniques by position, a glance at the rules of Touch might be in order.

There are rules and rules, of course, starting with two-

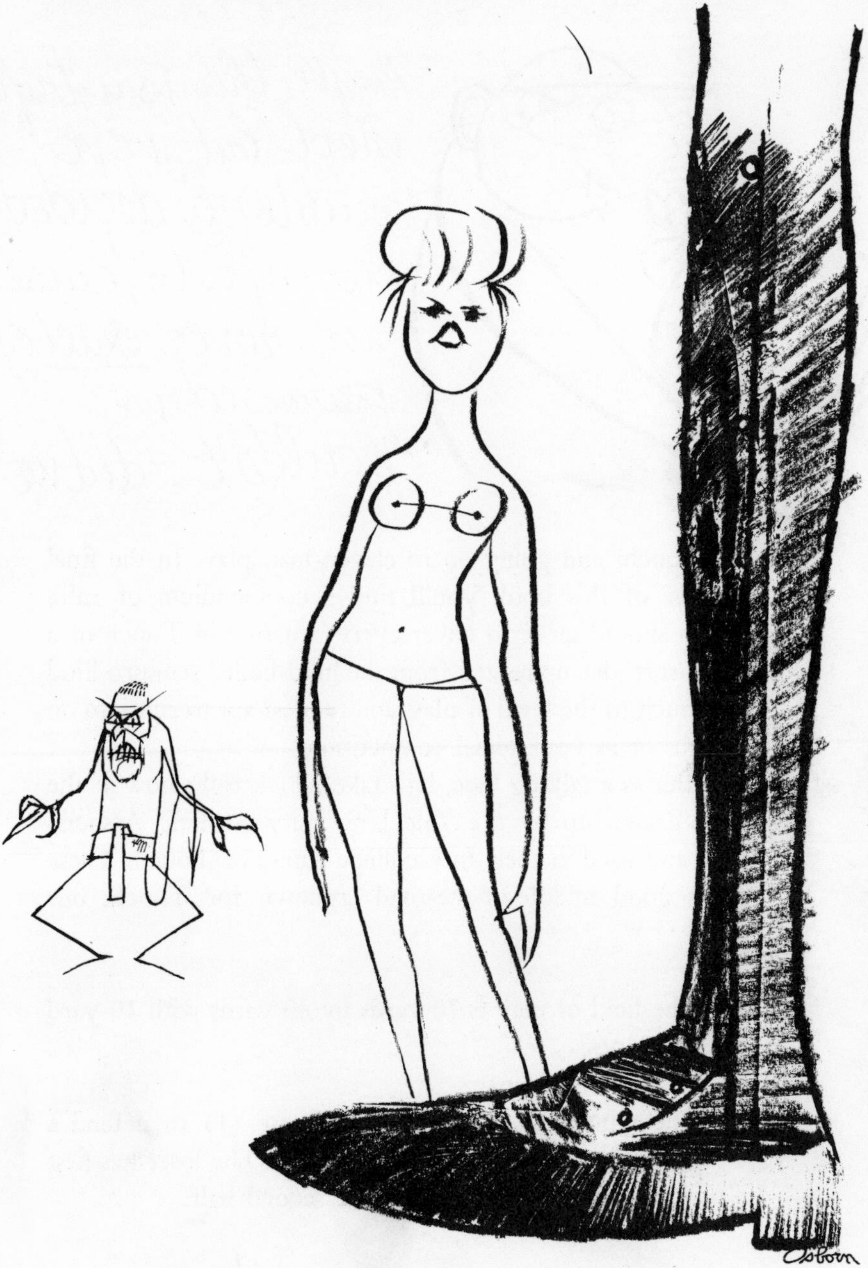

Maybe this is a trifle inept but we've suddenly decided to inflate, 'cause we never exactly promised we wouldn't ... did we?

man touch, and going on to eleven-man play. In the final chapter of this book you'll find a compendium of rules which should serve to cover every situation in Touch of a social sort, deemphasized from the hard-boiled semipro kind of Touch to the level of play you're most apt to run into on campus or in your social competitions.

But as a talking base, let's take a look right now at the rules drawn up by the Yale University Athletic Association, and used in their Intercollege games of Touch. These are a good middle-of-the-road laydown for Touch, our style:

1. The field of play is 70 yards by 40 yards with 10-yard end zones.
2. Six men on a team.
3. The winner of the toss may choose (1) to defend a goal; (2) to kick off; (3) to receive. The loser has first choice at the beginning of the second half.

4. Twenty plays to a quarter (kickoffs do not count)—change goals at the end of the first and third quarters. Tie games—no overtime period.

5. The team that kicks off may do so in any manner from its own 20-yard line. Ball must go past middle of field before it can be recovered by kicking team.

6. No tackling.

7. No interference.

8. A team has five downs in which to score.

9. A down is over when:
   a. The ball carrier is tagged by an opponent;
   b. Forward and backward passes touch the ground;
   c. The ball is out of bounds (kickoff out of bounds must be kicked over).

10. The ball is put in play at the spot:
    a. Where the carrier is tagged;
    b. From which an incomplete pass was thrown—provided the pass was beyond the line of scrimmage;
    c. Of the preceding down if an incomplete pass was thrown from behind the line of scrimmage;
    d. From which an incompleted backward pass was thrown;
    e. In the middle of the field opposite the point where the ball went out of bounds.

11. On the fifth down the offensive captain must state whether or not he will kick. If he kicks, he may do so without being rushed by the defensive team, but must wait until the defensive team is in position to receive the kick. Offensive team must hold its position until ball is kicked.

12. Both teams must be on sides.

13. The center must pass the ball backward from a position on the ground.
14. The ball must be passed forward or backward or laterally as many times as desired on any one play until it becomes dead—except on a kick it may not be passed forward.
15. Scoring is either by touchdown (6 points) or safety (2 points). The team against whom a safety is scored must kick the ball from its own 20-yard line.
16. The word of the tagger must be taken in determining whether or not he touched a runner.
17. The word of the passer must be taken in determining whether or not he released the pass before being touched.
18. Plain-soled shoes must be worn.
19. A fumble on a kicked ball will be declared dead at the point where the ball touches the ground.
20. The above rules are the exceptions to the official football rules.

I happen to like these rules for a nice free-and-easy Bethesda type of game, but if any parts of them don't appeal to you, a comparison with other systems given in Chapter Four will give you a basis for drawing up a set of your own. Some rules, for example, permit a one-handed tag. Others run four downs as in tackle football, with the quarters measured in terms of "time in" during actual play. These are simply a matter of preference.

There's one thing sure. Always play with a printed set of rules and an umpire to apply them. One of the basic truths of Touch, known as Lippincotter's Law (after the renowned jurist who settled all arguments on the field by

referring to a small black book which he always carried
with him, ostensibly a book of Touch rules but in actuality
an English-Icelandic dictionary carefully cupped in his
large hands) is that, without a standard, the decision inevitably goes to the hottest heads, the loudest shouters, or to
The Influentials, which is a pretty fair description of most
anyone interested in Touch, so a commonly accepted
Rulebook is indicated from start to finish.

The major aspects of this game are the pass, the tag,
the kick, the run, and the block. Before you play Touch,
it might be well to review what the proper techniques are
in these divisions.

The Pass

A good passer, usually the quarterback, can mean
much to the team. But everyone should be able to pass accurately, especially at the short ranges that abound in
Touch.

The overhand grip is best. This is the kind you see
the pros use most of the time. What you're really doing
here is *grabbing* about one-half of the ball and throwing
it as if it were a baseball. The other half of the ball has
to go along, naturally, unless you're playing with a really
antique pigskin. There are some footballs made smaller
especially for Touch and these increase the importance of
the overhand grip.

The little finger of your right hand (or throwing
hand) is placed on the third horizontal lacing of the football, pointing one end up. The ring finger is an inch away,
the middle finger spread about an inch away from that so
that the index finger falls almost on the point of the ball.
The thumb grasps the ball on the other side, closing with

its force toward the index finger more than the others.
You're *squeezing* this apple now. The index finger is the
key finger in aiming and throwing it.

This grip takes a little practice, but is best in the long
run. If you're not at home with it, however, or find that
your hands are not big enough to grasp the ball in the
overhand grip, you'll want to palm it.

The palm grip is the easiest way of all. You simply
cradle the ball in your palm, with the laces touching the
tips of your fingers, and then you roll it off your palm
and spiral it into its flight.

There are other grips, but these two are really all you
need to know for Touch.

In throwing with the overhand grip, you'll toss the
ball almost like a baseball pitcher—cocking the ball at the
ear, and shooting it out with a long, straight, overarm delivery.

You can do the same with the three-quarter, or throw-
ing-rocks-at-frogs-in-a-pond, delivery, which takes off at
about shoulder level with the ball held just above the biceps
of the throwing arm. This is probably the most natural one
for normal Touch players, but it lacks some of the zing
and accuracy of the overhand.

The palm grip may be, you'll find, the best one for the
long, lazy, hell-and-gone pass for the touchdown. You get
a full-arm chance to get the ball back there, and a Ferris-
wheel motion to get it high into the air with plenty of force
to carry it far. A good player can throw just as far overhand, but for average passers, the palm is best for distance.

While we're thinking about passing, don't forget several other versions worth practicing so that they come
easily on the field.

There's the side-arm pass—bending over and throwing from about waist high at your side, you can rifle a pass through the crowd now and then from this unexpected position.

The underhand pass, tossing it in a scooping motion, is the best for short, unexpected laterals.

In an extremity—but don't use it too often, or they'll come to expect it—you can pass off to yourself. This should be done while running at very high speed, waiting for the moment of an unavoidable tag, and then passing over the heads of your taggers and catching your toss with a burst of extra speed. In some rules, this isn't allowed. However, it's a lot of fun and maybe you'll want to give it clearance to get extra possibilities into your game.

Lastly, every player should be able to pass while in motion. The quarterback may want to stand and get set at certain times to gauge the way the play is developing, or to ready himself for a few forward steps to put extra motion into his long pass. But as play develops, each man must accustom himself to passing while running at top speed and doing it accurately. The old principle of leading the target—so useful in aerial gunnery and so beautiful in execution when it's done right—goes into play here. The speed of your body motion is added if you're throwing straight ahead; is subtracted *in toto* if you throw backward; and if you're throwing out to any angle, you have to allow for the carry-through past the spot selected by your eye which is contributed by your body motion. Put this into practice by running with the ball, and throwing at a tree trunk or a telephone pole. After you've learned how to draw a mental parallelogram of forces with respect to your speed and motion, you'll begin to acquire the ability to throw an ac-

curate pass. After that, it's up to your natural coordination and strength in reaching and hitting your target.

There's quite an art to catching a pass, too. It takes a good 'pair of hands and a deftness that certainly can't be transmitted by the contagion of print. Nevertheless, there are a few fundamentals you won't want to forget, even if you know them.

If you're running on a set play, to a given point, of course you're not even going to look back at the passer and give the play away. But if you're merely improvising, you should wigwag your intentions to him. If you're in the clear, turn and face both open hands to him, giving him a fair target. Probably you won't be—so you're better off to signal with one hand where you'd like the play. Usually it should be about five yards away, so that while the pass is in the air, you're running toward it.

In catching any pass, remember the word *give*. A long high one calls for a basket catch, in which you let the ball descend in front of you as you run, and then ease it down into the basket made by your hands, palms up, and forearms held as close together as the width of the ball at its narrowest. If you're really big-handed, you can just grab the pass with your fingers, and there'll be many times you'll have to do just that, especially on short hard ones. Even then, however, you'll want to cushion the catch a bit by giving, so that the ball doesn't just bounce back off your rigidly held fingers.

The Tag

Most respectable games of Touch require a two-handed tag, since this seems to be the Touch equivalent of the tackle which stops the runner in regular football. The tag is always made with the open hands, palms down.

One football authority suggests that the tagger throw up both arms immediately to signal the point of the tag, thus preventing the runner from staggering on ten more feet or so before stopping to acknowledge that he's been tagged. That seems a little extreme for the kind of Touch were talking about. So does the rule permitting a tag anywhere on the body. We must remember that the tag is always made with a firm definition. If you're playing opposite a behemoth with a pair of Westphalian hams instead of hands, and he spends the afternoon crashing them down (well coated with blood, sweat, and tears) on your bald pate as a sign that he's caught up with you again, you're going to harbor dark and vengeful thoughts every time you get the ball. Equally, since Touch does have its elements of danger, that possibility is increased if tags are allowed on the legs or calves. It makes for a sort of half-tackle, a tripping and crashing motion that can upset a player and really upend him besides. The two-handed tag between the waist and the Adam's apple is best for most games, and you'll find adequate satisfaction in getting to the laying on of hands with a will—your opponent is doubly annoyed to be caught and to get a solid thumping between the shoulder blades and on the chest, besides.

In some games, they use a tag-flag, a strip of cloth which is worn tucked under each player's belt, and whipped out by the opponent near enough to do so, instead of a tag. This may be all to the good, but to someone suddenly coming on the fracas, it looks more like the Rape of the Sabine Women or a college panty raid than anything else. It also suggests that every player in the game is such a liar that a tag can't be registered without a banner waving in the breeze to prove it. The Yale rules, implying that the word of any Blue is worth taking in the matter of a tag, would seem to be sufficient. Otherwise, get some new friends. When girls are playing Touch, you'll do well to give yourself a brisk lecture before the game—either to intercept passes thrown to them, or tag exclusively on the dorsal side. The other way may not lead to actual explosions, but at the very least to disaster and unexpected advertisements not privy to this high-minded pursuit.

All in all, the tag should be made cleanly, firmly, but without unnecessary roughness. Tripping, grabbing the opponent by the hair with one hand while you tag him with the other, shoving someone in his path, or rolling an oil drum at him to distract his line of thought are all fouls. Actually clobbering a little guy for the sheer joy of hurting him, even with a clean two-handed tag, is unsporting, unless of course, he is interested in your girl. Let *noblesse oblige* rule, I say—which means—watch out for yourself and let the other guy do the same.

The Kick

Since all the rules call for playing Touch without any special equipment whatsoever, including kicking shoes, you may want to go easy on this department. If you're inclined to think that anyone with a set of toes sheathed in a $1.98 pair of sneakers can boot a ball fifty yards on a kickoff, you might start off by giving a few preliminary boots to the base of the Washington Monument. You'll feel another shaft—of pain—that'll run right off the points of your pretty earlobes, and your foot, unwrapped, will resemble one of those frozen packages of lobster parts, a study in bright red and dead white.

Hence I suggest either that you find some primitive type on your side who enjoys using his foot as a launching pad, and to hell with the concatinated toes, or that you punt the ball on the kickoff. If this is dangerous, because you haven't got a kicker who can really get the distance, you might produce a Lippincotter ruling that you're allowed to open the action by throwing a long pass to the opposition. And, if you haven't got a long passer, complain about a sudden pain in your spleen, go to the nearest saloon for a moment of refreshment and contemplation, and then seek out the nearest air-conditioned movie for the afternoon.

On a kickoff, the ball may be placed on the ground and held by one of your team in the kicking position. He sets it on end, like Columbus making his point about the egg. He does not hold up the game by trying to flatten the ball by tapping it on the ground, but places his index finger delicately at the top of the ball, with the long axis vertical. All the tackle-football rule books recommend that he crouch on one knee and turn his face toward the opposing goal. This apparently is to suggest that that is where the ball will come down, and also to avoid any flinching when the kicker comes roaring in and lets him have one on the side of the head. Also, if his index finger is to be severed by the kick and to go into flight with the ball, it all comes as a delightful surprise.

The kicker then paces off the number of steps—say six or seven—required to give him good running speed and a free-swinging boot at the ball, and down he comes. He tries, of course, for depth above all. Failing that, he attempts to kick the ball into the left corner and away from the receivers, although the latter is not too possible in Touch, since all hands are ready to catch it, unconcerned with setting up blocks or forming moving defense patterns. (The left corner is suggested chiefly because most runners do best on their right side and so this automatically cramps their style.)

The punt is used much more frequently, and very much as in regular football. Right here we won't discuss the tactics, however, but simply how it's done.

The kicker takes three steps before booting it. If he's

right-footed, then it's short left—medium right—long left—
and kick, with increasing momentum being built up to a
maximum effort of the kick.

You hold the forward part of the ball in your left hand,
angling the ball to the left, and lowering the front of the
ball somewhat. The right hand steadies the ball from the
top rear, almost as if you are going to give it a shove, like
launching a canoe. The laces are up, unless you fancy getting a nice bit of pattern work on your instep when you
kick the ball.

The ball is held waist-high, directly over the kicking
leg.

The important thing about punting is that you must
virtually kick the ball out of your hands, actually catching
it with your instep just as it is released and pendant in the
air. Don't *drop* it onto your foot—I've seen a punter do
that from behind his own goal line and kick one straight
up into the air. (It was ring-around-the-rosie after that,
with twenty-two men under the ball, and a touchdown or
a safety in store for the score, depending on which team
caught it. The ball, on that occasion, squirted merrily
from one pair of outstretched hands to the other, and
finally settled down for a safety.)

You do not, of course, kick with your toes but with
the instep. The ball fits nicely into that curvature, and you
bend your toes downward to improve that. You catch the
ball with the instep toward the aft end, and if you've put it
all together in the right way, she'll sail. If you haven't
punted a football for a while, or never have, you'd better
practice up a little. The secret is not entirely in strength
or effort, but—as in most sporting gestures—in coordination
and in the proper application of your own body and leg

momentum to the immobile object.

It is important to remember that in Touch the kicker signals his punt, and members of the opposing team are not allowed to cross the line of scrimmage until after the ball has been kicked. This protects the kicker at all times, and also eliminates the quick-kick.

The Run

Here again, I'll discuss the tactics of this in another paragraph on backfield duties, but for the moment there are a couple of points to remember which apply exclusively to Touch.

First, don't tuck the ball close to your body as in tackle football. Nobody's going to jar your teeth loose with a tackle or a running block and even if you drop the ball, Touch rules restore it to your own team immediately at the spot where it fell. Therefore, run with it in your hand, away from the body, in whatever position you need to help you best in your balance or in achieving maximum speed.

Second, if you have a chance, hold the ball in your passing grip. Obviously this will be an advantage as your opponents bear down on you and you have seconds only in getting the ball away to one of your teammates.

The Block

In seven-man and eleven-man Touch, there is some reason to permit blocking with two-men-on-one, in order to open up holes in the line, and so forth. Those in the game may decide whether they want to go in for this aggressive type of play or not. Generally speaking, it would seem OK in organized league play in which competition is extremely keen, but it is probably too rugged for purely social Touch. One-on-one is about right.

There's another critical decision to make on blocking and this has to do with downfield blocking.

In Touch, the block is made in the line by crossing the arms against the chest, closing the fists, and then making a bodily drive against the chest of the opponent—always above the waist—to prevent him from rushing in and tagging the passer or runner. In this block, the main force is exerted by getting in the way, or perhaps by pushing the defensive linesman back and out of the play. The defensive linesman, particularly if he is a smaller guy, may occasionally take to eye-gouging, pinching, tickling, or inserting pebbles in the ears of the blocker in order to divert him from his earnest efforts. But normally he will push him back or run around him.

Under no circumstances may the Touch blocker leave his feet, flinging his body at the opposing linesman in an effort to divert him. Flinging your own body at someone who would like nothing better than to step on or over it is a stupid kind of offering anyway in an amateur game, and if the instinct arises within you, try doing it in front of a subway train. At least you may get a line or two in the newspapers that way.

Well, in some games of Touch, downfield blocking of the same sort is allowed to carve out a passage for the runner, but since this can be exceptionally dangerous—most of the injuries in tackle football result from moving blocks—Touch rules require a standing block. The offensive player comes to a halt and applies his block as he would in the line.

Rugged characters can get plenty of fun applying

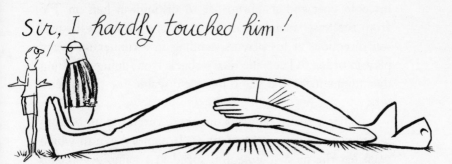

Sir, I hardly touched him!

blocks in the line, or setting up a protection in the backfield for the passer through a series of standing blocks, and this should be sufficient to send the hot red blood coursing through their healthy little veins. This provides them with quite a bit of bodily contact play, but since Touch is primarily a game devoid of contact, there should be a sensible limit placed on it. Therefore, there should be careful scrutiny of all downfield blocks, to make sure that they are positively "standing."

In our section on tactics, we'll discuss how the block can be made a valuable ingredient in a scoring play.

And so, from techniques to tactics.

General Tactics

The practitioners of regular football, like those of war, enjoy overemphasis on their skills. Any general in charge of an army may advance, retreat, stand still, or attempt to encircle his enemy on either flank—and that is about all. There is nothing much else for him to do, except keep his supplies up and try to figure out what his opponent has in mind.

The football coach is faced with an equally simple

problem. Having trained his team, more or less, he puts on his polo coat and snapbrim hat to distinguish him on TV from the lesser members of his staff, and proceeds to snarl out directions at his players, sending in a runner on every play in order to keep the quarterback from doing anything that might make the game more enjoyable for the spectators.

What actually happens out there often has no bearing whatsoever on his coachly fancies. It comes down to which team has the most muscle and speed in a game devoted to removing everybody in your way by every legal means. There are amusing similarities to war. In war, although you may sink an enemy ship and cast two thousand men into a sea of burning oil, no one ever really objects in a formal way. It is only when you pick up a few charred survivors and fail to ply them immediately with hot coffee and doughnuts that the word "inhumane" comes into play by the horrified rule makers and people who meet at Geneva. If you capture a general, you salute him, in deference to his rank: if you capture a private, you kick him, in deference to his lowliness. By any sensible reasoning, you would shoot the general immediately, as the greater nuisance, and free the private to go back and eat more of his army's food. In football, it is often considered sporting to knock a man down and then offer him a hand in getting back to his feet. The coaches, who know in their hearts that they are orators at best, usually stroll across the field after the game to congratulate each other on how hard the students played. This wonderful self-deception keeps everyone in a good humor, of course, in battle as well as in football, but it obscures the fact that sportsmanship in both arenas is the lowest form of cowardice. The gracious winner actually expects to lose next time, and is already putting in a bid for lenient treatment. That is why the generals of all nations were very upset over the Nuremberg trials. If the winners are going to kill the losers after every war, it's going to take all the fun out of it.

All this relates quite closely to Touch. Generally speaking, there has been far too much written about how you can advance a ball either by running it or throwing it to one of your teammates. Many charts are drawn up, and a tortured technical vocabulary invented to describe these cabalistic directives.

I think it seemly to approach our game with the same sense of realism displayed by President White of Cornell late in the last century. At that time some of his under-graduates wanted to travel to Cincinnati, Ohio, to play a team from Michigan on neutral ground. President White refused his boys permission, saying: "I will not permit 30 men to travel 400 miles merely to agitate a bag of wind." Football has never been put down better.

If we realize that we are about to play a game of foot-ball, but without tackling, and that is that, everyone will be happier. There are certain fundamental rules that will add slightly to that happiness, but not too many of them be-long here. Books and whole libraries have been written about how to play football, when every player actually knows that you learn best by going out there and doing it. However, I feel that certain things need to be said at this point, and if you find them revoltingly self-evident and downright insulting, I suggest that you tread skippingly over this advice and move on to Chapter Four, where you will find a compendium of rules, suitable for man or beast. But for those interested in the *curiosa* of finer play at

Touch, here are a few thoughts to ponder. I will begin first by discussing the requirements of the various positions in Touch, and then get on to the way they may be applied to team play.

Center: Offense

In regular football, although there are a few terrier types and rangy men with power and stamina, the center is usually a solid citizen with a peculiar point of view. That is, he spends a lot of his time looking backward through his legs, or glaring straight ahead into the eyes of an opposing linesman who has every intention of pulverizing him the minute the ball is snapped. His other point of view is looking up from the ground, after the opposing linesman and a couple of his buddies finish the job. If you watch the center after each play, you'll notice that he has three characteristic gestures. First, he straightens his helmet, which was pushed askew as someone tried to throttle him in the bottom of the pile-up; second, he checks on his front teeth to see if that parade over his face dislodged anything; and third, he looks around to see what happened on the play. Someone ought to send him a telegram, he's so far out of it.

The platoon system has pushed the offensive center even further into his unimaginative category. Defense centers are now free-ranging heroes: the offensive center is still a plodder who shoves the ball through his legs no matter what time it is, what the score is, and whatever he may be thinking.

Our man Martin Chuzzlewit is perfect for the job. Chuzzlewit is pudgy. (One must never call a football player fat, since they are always filled out with additional padding and so seem to live up to the inevitable "husky.")

This is perfect for Touch, and his intense desire to be as fleet as a hare also makes him the ideal pass receiver on a surprise play by an alert quarterback.

Let us examine what is expected of Chuzzlewit, the offensive center:

Unless he has been a center in regular football and able to pass the ball back through his legs with a reasonable degree of accuracy, Chuzzlewit will do a lot better to face the enemy, turning slightly to his left as he hands off or throws the ball to his quarterback, who is in position some 2 or 10 feet behind him, depending on the formation being used. In regular football, he would be smeared, of course, in this unorthodox position. But since he can't be tagged when he hasn't got the ball, and the play doesn't start until he gets rid of it, he's perfectly safe in assuming any position he wants. He may even, if he wishes, turn fully around and face his own quarterback, just tossing him the ball like an old apple. Nobody's going to hit him from behind in this game so he's safe enough for the time being. The forward position is recommended, however, since Chuzzlewit is, after all on the offense, and should get on down the field and make ready for a pass.

Since he is built along the lines of a bar of fudge, and got that way munching on a lot of it, no one anticipates that Roger Blough is going to be tossing any all-or-nothing passes to Chuzzlewit. However, Martin operates on the offense as an excellent threat. There are two plays in particular in which he may function in a major attack.

If the opposition is playing a zone offense, he is in an excellent position for a short flat pass from Roger, right over the center position, with Martin about 10 yards down the field. From that point, after catching his pass, he may lateral to one of the fast halfbacks—perhaps both Brigitte and Krishna are now hotfooting it down their respective sidelines—and Chuzzlewit can pass, or even hand off to them on a crisscross play, if that is in the wind.

This type of play is used infrequently but often with effect, shooting for short sure gains down the middle while the opposition is watching more carefully for scoring passes to the ends or middle-depth passes to the halfbacks. Chuzzlewit, in other words, can never be a hero but he can be useful, which is quite an accomplishment when you consider his natural abilities.

The other play in which Martin can win friends and influence the scoring is by tailgating, somewhat as they do in basketball, when the #1 man, closely guarded, suddenly flips the ball back over his shoulder to a tailgater who carries through on the play without losing a step. On the Touch variation of this, Chuzzlewit moves rather slowly into the area where—let us say—Roger Blough has instructed Truman Capote to rendezvous for a pass. Truman may catch it and go on his merry way. But let us assume that he has had to buttonhook back to get it, or that a higher trajectory than expected was slowing him down and making him wait too long for it. He may catch it, therefore, but be open to an almost immediate tag. Therefore, the play is planned so that he catches it and immediately passes off to Chuzzlewit, who is now thundering along, having fooled his guard by lollygagging on the way and then letting go with a burst of speed close by Capote. Truman may even, if he wishes, pass the ball backward to Martin in a set pattern, precisely as in basketball. It's a good play, and is really keyed to Chuzzlewit's relatively unthreatening position just after he has passed the ball to Blough. The halfbacks have a running start on him, and his own ends have the best chance of all to get on down the field. Hence he may be regarded as the least dangerous of all in advancing the ball, and this is all to the good on such a play.

If he were to take the pass from Capote, let us say, well on the right side of the field, it might be planned that Blough would be moving down the left sideline (after throwing his pass to Capote) and possibly already past his own defensive opponent. If that were the case, Martin could let loose from his point with an almighty heave toward the goal and Blough might take it in as simply as hiking the price of raw steel.

The Ends

Truman Capote and the Archbishop play these important positions, and it's lucky that they happened on the field during the choosing up of sides because both are superbly fitted for their difficult assignments.

Being an end requires speed, stamina, imagination, and the innate ability to make much out of something very unpromising, such as a short, wobbly pass or one thrown out of the reach of ordinary mortals.

If you are running to catch a pass, never make a gallant try and then drop it. If, in your judgment—particularly if you are a member of the Supreme Court—you can't quite catch it, show signs of strain in your face, slow down, and thus make the passer look bad.

The end may occasionally be deployed in to protect the backfield on a running play with a standing block, but most of the time he is the team's greatest offensive weapon. Ideally, his speed is under control, and easily convertible

into fast breaks to one side or another, buttonhooks to re-verse his field, and the like, which confuse the opposition and put his pass-catching talents to work in the outfield.

The end knows that his opposite expects him to catch a pass: opponent therefore has one thing in mind, and one thing only, to stick along and be on hand for the intercep-tion or the tag when the ball arrives.

The end, thus, must apply deception before catching the ball, and this is his second biggest job. Both Capote and the Archbishop must be experts in certain basic field ma-neuvers such as the following:

As mentioned earlier, the *Down-and-Out* pass, or Hell-for-Leather throw, is certainly not one that the Archbishop would be expected to catch. But the Capotian mood, as established in *Breakfast at Tiffany's*, seems perfectly attuned to a successful handling of this pitch.

This is the simplest gambit of all in the passing vocabulary. The end heads downfield, relying on his deception and speed to outwit the defenders. The quarterback lets go with his mightiest throw, and the end does his mightiest to catch it. It involves skills far beyond what this meager description suggests, but that is the gist of it—outrun the defenders, catch the pass on the other side of them, and keep going.

We permitted the Archbishop to specialize in the Buttonhook pass, because of his penchant for gaiters, and we add to this the Buttonhook-and-Eye.

In this, the good prelate scuttles downfield for some yardage, giving the impression that he's on a Down-and-Outer. Naturally, the defenders fade a bit to allow for his speed, and to prevent him from getting on the goal side of them. Then, he simply draws up and pulls back to the pass which Blough deliberately tossed short of him.

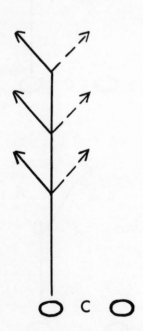

In the Buttonhook-and-Eye, the Archbishop develops the deception of his straight buttonhook run by branching off either to the right or left, as decided in the huddle, to catch a middle distance pass, pulled back deliberately but angled for open territory.

The Warp-and-Woof pattern, as recommended for an end, is certainly one for the novelist rather than the churchman, since a tracing of the end's path on this maneuver suggests that he may be full of Martinis. The idea here is to zigzag in his running and thus deceive until the last minute any defenders who may try to cut him off, based on a conjecture over his general direction.

Both Truman and the Archbishop are suitable proponents of the Siva Shape pass, in which the cutaway tactic is used. The end goes down midfield, with a choice of depth as to when he cuts over to the sideline. The defenders know this, of course, but never know at what point the cut will be made— 10, 12, 15, or 20 yards deep. The offensive end simply checks with the quarterback as to which distance he'll elect, and they both count it off in seconds as the end runs on down.

The Ben Turpin pattern involves both Capote and the Archbishop.

They head straight down after the ball is snapped, then crisscross to each other's side of the field to receive the pass. They can fake the cross, of course, further Turpinizing the opposition by returning to their original sides—and any alternatives thereof. The important thing is to have their pattern work out in conjunction with the quarterback's pass.

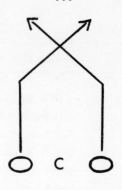

The Vestpocket Turpin is a variation of this, in which Truman and the Archbishop cross close to their own lines, playing for a short pass rather than a deep one.

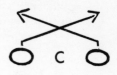

The Belmont, or Run-for-the-Wire tactic, is based upon the simple mathematics of space which every jockey knows—if you can get your horse on the rail, particularly on that all-important last turn, you'll force everyone else to run farther as well as faster to pass him. On the Belmont tactic, the end merely gets a wide piece of the field and keeps curving to make his defender run a few more steps than he in order to get the tag. The quarterback, forewarned as to the direction of the Belmont maneuver, leads with his pass, and puts the defender at least a few paces in the minus column.

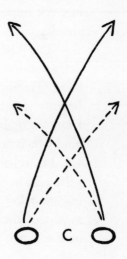

The final technique for the end to employ is the Stanislavsky method of fooling the opposition. He may kneel for a moment, obviously winded, before the play on which he knows he is about to make a 50-yard break at top speed. They will expect anything, presumably, but a play to this physical wreck. He may deliberately throw out a few warning gestures on unimportant plays—such as tightening the shoelaces, wiping the brow, and so on—in order seemingly to tip off the defenders as to his being the pass-catcher. Later, on a much more critical play, disregarding the previous well conditioned tipoffs, he merely stands back on his heels, observes the cuticle and half-moons of his fingernails, and couldn't seem to care less. Then he'll really outwit the oppostion—unless they've read this book.

The Halfbacks

Krishna and Brigitte, the halfbacks, are the all-around members of the team. They block, they run, they pass.

If their own linemen have done a decent job on blocking, the opposing center, and ends, will be delayed on the attack.

The halfback who is on the offense, is momentarily defense-minded if his quarterback is about to perform the basic Touch play of passing to the ends. Krishna and Brigitte, therefore, stand rocklike in a triangle pattern in front of their passer, forming the sides of a fortress behind which he flings.

On other plans discussed in the strategy section, the halfbacks become the key running or passing units by taking a handoff from the quarterback and function thereafter as part of the repassing combination which the whole team now assumes.

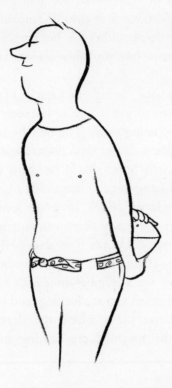

Halfbacks may take the pass from Chuzzlewit just as the quarterback may, to vary the offense pattern.

On still other plays, the ends may turn back to serve as blockers for the passer, while the halfbacks go on downfield, interchanging duties with the ends, and utilizing their same deception tactics to outwit the defense.

The Quarterback: Offense

I could not attempt to bring into this slender volume the harsh realities of quarterbacking, since experts in the science have devoted whole books to it with only a slight communication of skill. Here, we will go on the assumption that the quarterback is already familiar with the tactics of football, or he wouldn't be bucking for this job, and simply feed him a few probably unnecessary reminders.

1. The quarterback, being no Oracle of Delphi, has no Sibylline wisdom to guide him in his search for the weaknesses of the opposing team. The best he can do is to keep tapping away like a doctor who doesn't know what is really the matter but who hopes that if he keeps at it long enough something will *bong* out of tune inside or there will be the rattle of a displaced chunk of bone somewhere. So the quarterback devotes a play or two to tapping out the physiology of the enemy. On the first play, perhaps, he goes for the touchdown—testing their reaction to the element of surprise. He mixes up a number of passes to see where the wooden-legged defenders are lurking, and he diagnoses during these tentative plays where the dreamers, the overanxious, and the spavined are lurking in the opposition fold.

2. Given the chance, he has schooled his own team in a number of basic plays, which they know pretty well. He works his trick plays on these basics by devising variations in the huddle and explaining to his men what the special maneuver will require of them. By and large his basic plays will consist of:

   a. About ten pass patterns based on the ability of ends and halfbacks to get into a recognized area at a prescribed number of seconds after the ball is snapped.

   b. A fake pass play or two, consisting of handoffs, the Statue of Liberty play, and the like, taking advantage of the running room an apparent pass setup will provide.

c. A spread pass formation in which his line fans out across the field, drawing the defenders with them, and opening up holes both for passing and running through the formation.

d. A series of T-formation plays in which he operates just behind center, and swiftly sets up offensive patterns by passing or handing off to his ends and halfbacks, either for run-on-down plays, or to steal a second or two for them to pass.

e. A series of single-wing plays, with one halfback close to the line behind an end, the other halfback deep. This sets up an extra man downfield for a pass, with the other halfback coming on through fast for a lateral, or for actually tossing the pass. The variations on this, with the quarterback only a few yards behind the center, also permit end runs toward the weak side, for surprise, or end-arounds on the strong side aided by the extra blocking of the wingback.

3. The quarterback tries, as much as possible, to keep to a minimum the time that the ball is in the air on a pass play. He just can't loop those lazy, pretty jobs out there—they have to zip on through before the opposition has time to diagnose the play while the ball is sailing up there with the birdies.

4. The quarterback must, as every coach since 1880 has said, be a gambler. He knows, of course, that if you toss a coin in the air ten thousand times, the odds are always still the same—even—as to whether it will come down heads or tails, viewed from infinity. Viewed from the same vantage

point in a game of Touch, a quarterback who repeats a successful play may be just as vulnerable as the one who repeats an unsuccessful play, since the former is possibly just
complacency and the latter possibly a fine bit of generalship.
But if the heads-and-tails odds of his opponents' expectancy
work out against him, he will just seem like a poor guesser.
The good quarterback is the one who guesses right most
often.

5. The quarterback is also responsible for the language used
in the huddle. In order to get his team moving in unison, he
is required to utter caveman gutterals such as *hup* to break
up the huddle after he has announced the play, and *hike*
when he wants the ball snapped. This is reminiscent of the
military and gives the game a fine air when you're winning,
but a series of hups and hikes coming out of the mouths of
those some thirty points behind begins to sound asinine, so
it is best to keep these barks and yipes to as low as a decibel
count as possible, at least until the score begins to settle
down in your own favor.

6. Above all, in Touch, he must at all times have a play in
mind, even if it is the wrong play. The degeneration of the
game into one in which all the players run out for a long
pass all the time turns what can be a lively and competitive
tussle into a dull race for a piece of animal skin, a prospect
which begins to pall even after the third repetition. Variety
is still the spice of life and of Touch.

7. He should run with the ball as infrequently as possible.
The implication is that brains should never be confused with
exertion. Besides, he might get tagged.

Osborn

8. The quarterback must be, in the final analysis, a very gifted actor. To begin with, he must exude confidence, even though in his heart of hearts he has never dealt with such a hamstrung collection of dumbbell clashers in his whole life as this dispirited herd. He must also act as if every tag by the opposition were an outrageous accident of mischance which will be immediately corrected on the next play. He must also instill in his players certain emotional reactions which will tend to make them outdo their own puny abilities. Glowering looks, mutterings, snarls, and outright insult greet failure to catch a pass, even though the wobbly pumpkin he laid out there 25 yards short of the mark couldn't have been caught by a 9-foot end on the Green Bay Packers. If the pass is caught, he nods grimly, as if to say that here's the least someone should do in Touch, and whadda you expect, a medal? Even though this may be enough in itself to consign him to any sensible man's Purgatory, he must exude such a sense of dedication and virtue that his teammates are ashamed to evaluate him as anything less than a spark plug, a dynamo, a ball of fire, someone who's with it, and who, like the toad, wears yet a precious jewel in his head. Of such is the true quarterback made—which is why it may be all to the good that there is only one on a team.

Defensive Strategy

The tactics here are, of course, in almost every case a reply to the offensive planning discussed under the duties of the quarterback in the last section. The fact is that defense is as much inspiration as planning, and most players will discover this on the field. There are certain basic formations which are worth reviewing, however—these are still for the six-man game, and you may enlarge them with additional personnel for the bigger games.

The most sensible defense against a general running and passing attack is a zone defense in which each player takes up a position as soon as the ball is snapped and is responsible for defending within that area. The team covers the whole defense sector, so:

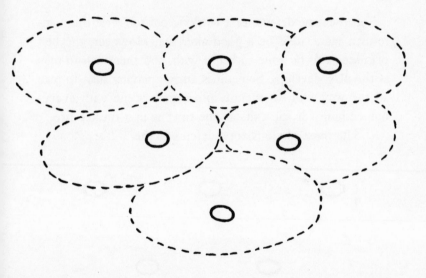

As soon as the ball is thrown, however, since that is the focus of each play, the defenders may drift out of their zones and into the activity area to give support to their man there, and to check off the possibility of laterals. At that point, if they have been playing strictly zone defense, they take on man-to-man assignments as follows:

Defensive	to	*Offensive*
quarterback		center
first halfback		right end
right halfback		left end
center		quarterback
right end		left halfback
left end		right halfback

If the zone defense isn't working out too well, this man-to-man tactic may be a good alternate. However, the best plan seems to be zone to begin with, and then man-to-man as the play develops. Sometimes a team playing man-to-man all the way will degenerate into a mob scene with everyone rushing for the exits at one time as in a theater fire.

The most obvious zone defense is the 3-2-1:

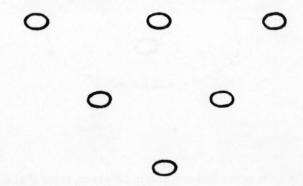

This is the defense to use against the T-formation and leaves Blough about twelve yards deep in his territory, with

Bardot and Menon about six feet behind the line.

Defense in punt formation is virtually the same, except that the backfield players go deeper—Brigitte and Krishna about twelve yards, and Blough about thirty yards from the line of scrimmage—depending upon the capacity of the kicker.

If you find yourself up against a single-wing offensive formation, there has to be some slight shift with it, so this is accomplished also with the 3-2-1, with this adaptation:

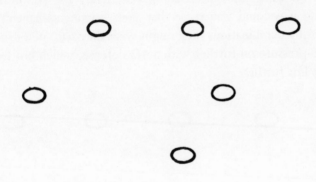

If the offense seems to be getting through your defense, there are a number of variations open to you. The 3-1-2 pattern, for example, throws your star defensive player into something of an additional roving center, alert to diagnosing plays, red-dogging the offense, or simply running down the ball. The pattern also leaves two players back as safety men to cover long passes, and therefore this may be the one to elect if your opponents have been sending their ends successfully past your safety man on the 3-2-1 position.

If things have been going very badly for you on running plays, and you sense that your opponents haven't the passing combinations they might wish they had, you can put the pressure on further with a 4-2 defense, which bottles up the line further:

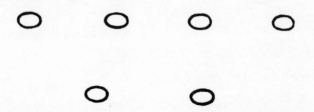

. . . and just as obviously, leaves your defense open for a strong passing attack.

The problem is always to outguess your opponents and to try and apply the defense for the particular play they're apt to try. Therefore, you won't assume your defense pattern until the ball is snapped. You call it in the huddle, then deploy as the play develops. If you want to be a little more sure of your guessing, you can start in the 3-2-1 pattern, then call *shift* to your team as the play develops, otherwise they may hold the standard positions.

On any kind of a spread play, you send your line out man-to-man to cover theirs:

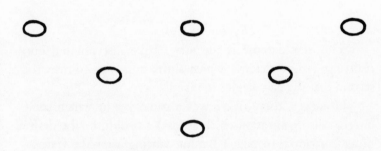

. . . and perhaps you'd want to bring your backfield into a 3-3 pattern if you're certain that your opponent is going to pass. The middle is open, naturally, on this gambit, so you'll be safer as a rule to keep your safety man deep and your halfbacks in closer to the line to safeguard against any attacks up the middle.

Receiving a Punt: Defense

The best lineup here is a 3-2-1, with your safety men spread out to cover any possible cornering of the kick. They should arrange in advance whether or not they will try a crisscross pass-off, or fake one, or lateral—the decision being indicated after the catch by enumerated signals with the fingers, according to the circumstances.

The #1 man plays in middle depth for a short kick, and the line linesmen function as blockers.

If you find that the opposition is getting downfield too fast on a punt, and that you're being throttled deep in your own territory, a shift to a 3-2-1 is recommended, especially if you have a good fast safety man who can catch a punt well. The extra manpower for blocking up front may serve to get more yardage than the other formation.

The same applies to the kickoff defense.

Defense by Position

The best defense is the one I have just pointed out, realizing a zone defense which shifts into man-to-man the second that the play begins to take shape.

However, there never was a game yet in which some internal disorganization—such as loss of breath, or the desire of a Chuzzlewit to take a Bardot dancing after the fracas—did not turn up, leaving the players on the field awaiting instructions that never come, like Marshal Ney making his epic charge against Blücher, not knowing of the disaster lying in the gully ahead of his hussars, uninformed by the Emperor's scouts.

These high-sounding references mean much more as you pound over the Touch field, wondering where in hell the ball is going to go next, and whatever happened to the voluble miracle man of only a few plays ago (he has now retreated into a pained silence, punctuated only by gasps and admonitions to those nearest him to "get in there"—a sharp decline in defense strategy). At this juncture in the game, only discipline (for example, a limit of four ounces of hard liquor before the game) and previous training (the knowledge that four glasses of sherry equal two Manhattans) can pull you through without losing face.

Herewith, therefore, face-saving data to apply while

your field general pulls himself together:

The end has to think fast and move fast. Generally speaking, his job is to rush the passer, and bowl over in the process any of the blockers who stand in his way, cuddling their tiny fists on their chests and sticking out their receding chins. If the play develops toward the center of the line, the end must choke in on it. If it seems to be reaching out, the end fades a little, forcing the play toward the sideline before he makes his bid for the tag. His job is to relieve the secondary defense of any problems except a deep pass—and that he will rush to pieces if he can. If his own center charges in to bowl over the offensive center, or to red-dog a ball carrier, one of the ends should drift back to cover the middle passing zone. This is a matter to decide in his own defensive huddle. Above all, the end must not let the play get around him. If he misses the tag but turns the play in, he has been at least a partial success.

The center, on defense, unless on a special misson, plays a roving freelance game. He watches for running plays, assists the secondary on pass defense, and watches his own middle defense zone for a flat short-distance pass. He varies these tactics as much as possible in order to prevent the offensive quarterback from noting a set pattern of defense play on his part.

The halfbacks, Debonnaires all, have eyes only for the ends. If they think Capote or the Archbishop is descending on them like the wolf on the fold, ready for a pass from Blough, their job is not complex but brutal. They must scuttle along, never letting the ends get between them and the goal line. They must either intercept the pass, break it up, or tag the successful pass-catcher. Interception is an art we couldn't possibly teach here or anywhere else. Breaking it up is half an interception—in any case, slap the ball into the ground, never up . . . and into the hands of some eager opponent. As for tagging, that'll do, of course, but a tag on the 2-yard line, however brilliantly executed, for some reason falls short of an event setting off dancing in the streets by an overjoyed populace.

The safety man, usually the quarterback, is in the most critical—and enjoyable—position of all on the defense. He is the three-headed dog at the gates, the Cerberus who prevents the ultimate entry. He never need commit himself on slashing interception runs such as the halfbacks must make, or ill-advised early rushes against a running play. His is a cornering job, a back-running insurance against the mistakes of others. Never will anyone rail at him for playing too deep. His is the court of last resort—no pass should be deep enough to go behind him. He watches with eyes sharpened by night watches on destroyers, by the sight of leopards on Kilimanjaro, by the heat of South American natives preparing sharpened coals to thrust into his orifices. In other words, he may be blind as a bat, but he has to act as if he sees everything. To do this, he runs from side to side of the field, always following the ball. He has the most responsible but easiest job of all. If he fades terribly deep and catches the runner or pass receiver, he's known as a sure-shot defense man. If he fades even deeper than that, and lets his halfbacks run themselves into Walter Reed Hospital covering a pass he should have long ago intercepted, he's recognized as a deep thinker, a scholar of the game, and a man of parts. In other words, always try to be the safety man. If you let them score on you, you're a bum. But most of the time they won't—and you can rest.

Triple threat man

Final Admonition

Accidents do happen, even in Touch, and it is a good idea to know in advance where a doctor may be reached. If possible, have him in the game as a player, which protects everyone except the medic himself.

Of course, if he breaks a leg, put him on the grass and get him talking about the evils of socialized medicine to take his mind off the pain. Meanwhile, his wife can get an interne over from the hospital and Doc can find out for himself just how much of a boon that can be.

Don't forget that when one of Napoleon's generals died during a foreign campaign, Napoleon shipped him back to Paris in a hogshead of rum to preserve the body. Meanwhile, they shipped the Emperor off to Elba and the hogshead was forgotten in the palace. When Napoleon made it back again to Paris, he looked up his old friend, and discovered that the General's mustaches had grown about seven feet in the interim and in the rum. The moral of this is that liquor and Touch do not mix. Never drink immediately after an injury is the best rule, especially if the injury resulted from a fall subsequent to knocking off a fast pint of whiskey.

Envoi

It has always seemed to me that the remark concerning the victory at Waterloo being won on the playing fields of Eton must have been singularly irritating to those of Wellington's men who spilled their blood on that foreign field, not realizing that the issue had already been decided on a peaceful school quadrangle.

In that sense, I feel deeply that Touch will do nothing to develop the character. It will not develop *esprit de corps*, since it reveals personal weaknesses and foibles in such a glaring light that you can hardly bear the faces of your best friends after only a few minutes of play. It will give no significance to your existence, since chasing a bladder from one end of a grassy sward to another and slapping others on the back can in no wise be construed as advancing the Christian ethic. It will not sharpen the edges of intellect.

It will make you sweat, though. It will make you run. It will make you leap. It will make you shout. It will make you breathe deeply. It will make you lie down gratefully. It will make you see your loved ones more fondly.

And it will lift your spirit, by some strange alchemy of ground, and sky, and purpose.

And how often in your everyday life does any one of these things happen?

So—you'd better play Touch.

Touch by the Numbers: Rules

I HAVE FREQUENTLY MENTIONED IN THE PRECEDING PAGES THAT EACH GROUP MAD ENOUGH TO HEAD INTO A GAME OF Touch should establish its own rules, according to the preferences and physical abilities of its members, and then appoint an umpire, preferably with the decisiveness and aggressiveness of a Tiglath-pileser.

As a guide in establishing this norm, the following standardized rules for playing Touch are included, in addition to those of the Yale Athletic Association given on page 00. A brief study of each will reveal certain variations which you can adapt to your own circumstances, in the formation of a rule book that will keep mayhem and misadventures to a minimum.

These rules have been drawn up by colleges in the forefront of the football scene. Variations are expected, as you may desire, and mutations may be necessary, to make Touch more enjoyable for you. All that's really necessary is to do it your way, as long as you do it.

Seven-Man Touch: as Played at Michigan State University
Dimension of field shall be 40 yards by 60 yards with a 10-yard end zone. Team must have seven men on the field within ten minutes of scheduled time or forfeit the game. Teams may continue a game with only six men. Managers must list starting time.

Kickoff

1. The kickoff may be made by punting or kicking off.
2. The kickoff is made from the 12-yard line.
3. The restraining line for the receiving team is the 20-yard line. Three men must remain between the 2–25 yard lines until the kick is made.
4. On a kickoff, if the ball is kicked beyond the receiving team's restraining line (20-yard line), the kicking team may recover the ball. The receiving team may advance the ball from the air or ground.
5. If a ball is kicked out-of-bounds inside of the receivers' 20-yard line, it is put in play by scrimmage on the 20-yard line. If the ball goes out of bounds outside the 20-yard line, it is put in play where it went out. Balls that go in or over the end zone will be put in play on the receivers' 12-yard line.

Position of Players

1. Both teams shall have seven members.
2. An offensive team shall have four men on the line of scrimmage and three men in the backfield. Line of scrimmage extends one foot from near end of ball. Defensive team may have no less than two men on line of scrimmage (exception—free kick: *see* Free Kick)
3. One backfield man may be in motion parallel to the line of scrimmage before the ball is snapped. Only one man may be in motion during one play.

Osborn

Passing

1. Any number of forward and lateral passes may be made on any play that starts from scrimmage.
2. No forward passes may be made on a play started by a kick (punt or kickoff). Any number of lateral passes are permitted.
3. The ball is put in play after an incomplete forward pass at the spot from which the pass was thrown except when the pass is thrown from behind the line of scrimmage. Pass caught over or outside end zone is an incomplete forward pass.
4. If the ball is thrown from behind the scrimmage line and is incomplete, the ball is put in play at the line of scrimmage.
5. No man may pass to himself either forward or laterally.
6. If a pass is intercepted, it may be thrown forward.

Fumbles

1. All fumbled balls are immediately dead. An incomplete lateral is put in play at spot of throw.
2. The ball is put in play at the spot the player dropped the ball.
3. Team fumbling ball will retain possession of the ball.
4. Any passed or fumbled ball that does not touch the ground may be advanced by any player catching it.

Touching

1. The ball is dead when the ball carrier is touched above the knees with either hand by a defensive player who is on his feet.
2. Ball that is run or kicked outside comes in 15 yards from sideline.

3. If runner goes up in air to pass, toucher *may not jump in front to block runner with his body*.

Free Kick

1. A free kick may be declared by the offensive team.
2. When a free kick is declared, the ball must be kicked and four men from both teams must be on the line of scrimmage until the ball is kicked.
3. No one can rush the kicker on a free kick.
4. A quick kick may be executed at any time.
5. On a bad pass from center, the ball is dead where it stops.

Blocking

1. No body blocks are allowed at any time.
2. Shoulder blocking is allowed only on, or in back of, the line of scrimmage.
3. All other blocking must be made with the blocker in an upright position and with his hands in contact with his body.

Penalties

1. The offended team may have its choice of the penalty or refuse the penalty.
2. Five-yard penalties:
   a. off side
   b. backfield in motion
   c. four men not on the line
   d. defensive holding
   e. more than 15 seconds in the huddle
   f. more than one time out per half
   g. forward pass on a punt or kickoff return
   h. eight men on field

Osborn

    i. passing to self
3. Fifteen-yard penalties:
    a. diving to touch
    b. pass interference by the offensive team (also loss of down)
    c. offensive holding
4. (A) Loss of ball at line of scrimmage or at point of greatest loss:
    1. body blocking (offensive team)

2. shoulder blocking downfield (offensive team)
3. clipping (offensive team)
4. tripping (offensive team)
5. unnecessary roughness (offensive team)

(B) Half distance to goal line from point of violation or at spot of greatest loss:

1. body blocking (defensive team)
2. shoulder blocking (defensive team)
3. clipping (defensive team)
4. tripping (defensive team)
5. unnecessary roughness (defensive team)—to include rough body contact between toucher and runner; touch must be made without blocking runner's path.
6. Disqualification:
   Unsportsmanlike conduct (only captain of team talks to officials). Officials' judgment final as to acts by players that merit ejection.
7. Pass interference by defensive team.
8. If time runs out on a play and a penalty is called, the play will be run over unless the offended team declines the penalty.
9. If an error is made by an official (quick whistle), the down will be replayed.

Time Outs

1. Each team is allowed one 30-second time out per half; clock will stop.
2. Officials' time out will be taken for injury, explanation, etc. Clock will stop.
3. No time out the last two minutes of either half.
4. Time out for extra points.

5. Clock is stopped for substitutions, officials' decisions, and touchdowns. The substitutions must be done quickly and the clock stopped only momentarily.

Playing Periods
1. Each quarter will be 8 minutes along with an optional minute between halves and no time between quarters.

Scoring
1. Touchdown .... 6 points
2. Safety .... 2 points (put in play on 12-yard line)
3. Point after touchdown. 1 point (attempted from 2-yard line)
4. Touchback .... 0 point (put in play on 12-yard line)

Tie Games

1. A sudden death period of four minutes will be played. If
no score, game is tie. The first team to score will be the
winner. The choice of kicking, receiving, or goal will
be determined by the flip of a coin.

Equipment

1. Rubber-soled shoes *only* are permitted.
2. Equipment such as helmets or shoulder pads are pro-
hibited.
3. Disqualified players cannot return to the game.

Substitution

1. Any number of substitutions may be made during a
game. Substitutes' names must be put on game sheet.

Downs

1. Four downs will be allowed for the length of the field.
2. The ball will change hands after the fourth down.

Seven-Man Touch: as Played at U.S. Naval Academy

a. *Opposing Teams.* Opposing teams should wear jerseys
of contrasting colors. No headgear or padding of any kind
shall be worn. Shoes other than regulation gym shoes shall be
worn only when issued to all teams as part of regular playing
equipment.

b. *Players and Substitutions.* A team shall consist of seven
players, one of whom shall be captain. At least three players
must be on the line of scrimmage when the ball is put into
play. In no case shall a team be permitted to compete with
less than seven players. A player may enter the game at any

time after reporting to the referee without penalty, providing his entry does not delay the game.

c. *Length of Game.* The game shall be played in four periods of 15 minutes each. There shall be a 2-minute rest period between halves. There shall be no rest period between the first and second, and the third and fourth periods.

d. *Time Out.* There will be no time outs granted either team. The referee may take time out when he deems it essential.

e. *Kickoff.* The kickoff shall be made from any point on the kicking team's 10-yard line. The ball may be punted. All players of the kicking team must be behind the ball and within bounds when the kickoff is made. The restraining line for the receiving team will be 10 yards from the point of the kick. If the kickoff goes out of bounds, it shall be kicked over. If the second kickoff goes out of bounds, the receiving team will put the ball in play at the center line

or opposite the point where it went out of bounds, which-
ever is closer to the kicking team's goal line.

Interference on the kickoff: The receiving team on the
kickoff shall not form group interference.

Penalty. 15 yards from spot of foul.

The touch football fumble does not apply to the kickoff. The kickoff is a free ball and may be recovered by the
kicking team as long as the kick travels 10 yards or more.

Fouls on the kickoff by the receiving team will be
penalized at the spot of the foul, with the exception of off-
sides and violation of the restraining line rule.

f. *Fumbles.* A fumble is not a free ball. It becomes dead at
the point where it touches the ground to the team last in
possession of the ball at the time the fumble occurred. This
rule also applies to a "muffed" or touched ball. The fumble
does not apply on the kickoff or on an announced punt by
the kicking team on the fifth down.

g. *Touching or Tackling.* A touch or tackle occurs when-
ever an opponent touches the ball carrier with both hands.
The ball shall be declared dead at the point where the touch
occurs. No part of the toucher's body, except his feet,
shall be in contact with the ground during the touch, or
attempt to touch. Pushing or striking the ball carrier will
be penalized as unnecessary roughness. If the referee should
be unable to see whether or not a runner has been tagged,
the word of the tagger must be taken as to whether or not a
touching occurred.

h. *Sidelines.* Plays ending up close to the sidelines will be
brought in 10 yards from the sidelines.

i. *Scoring.* The scoring shall be the same as in regular football.

j. *Blocking.* In blocking on the line, as well as in the open, no part of the blocker's body, except his feet or hands, shall be in contact with the ground when the block is made. Holding, clipping, illegal use of forearms, leaving the feet while blocking, striking or tripping are all considered personal fouls.

Penalty. 15 yards from the spot where the ball was put into play, the down remaining the same.

k. *Downs and Yardage.* A team shall be given 5 downs in which to score. If a score is not made in 5 downs, the ball goes over to the other team. After each score the team behind shall have the choice of which goal it will defend.

l. *Offside or Backfield in Motion.* The play is not called back until the ball is dead. However, if the referee blows his whistle, whether inadvertently or not, the ball is dead.

m. *Forward Passing.* The offensive team is permitted to make one forward pass during any one play, and this one pass may be made from any point of the field of play, without regard to a line of scrimmage. No forward passes are allowed on kickoffs or pass interceptions. Every member of both teams is at all times eligible to receive a forward pass. If a second forward pass is made on the same play, there shall be a penalty of 5 yards from the spot of the foul and loss of a down.

n. *Pass Interference.* Pass interference by the passing team will result in a penalty of 15 yards from the previous spot of down and loss of down. Pass interference by the defensive team will result in the pass being ruled completed at the spot of the foul, and the down will remain the same. The penalty for intentionally grounding a forward pass is 5 yards from the spot of the foul and loss of the down. The penalty

for defensive holding is 5 yards from the spot of the foul;
the down remains the same.

o. *Kicking.* A blocked kick not going beyond the scrimmage
line may be recovered and advanced by either team. The
penalty for roughing the kicker is 15 yards from the spot of
the down.

Fouls by the kicking or receiving team while the ball is
in the air are to be penalized from the spot of the previous
down.

On the fifth down, the team in possession of the ball
may announce their intention to kick. Once the intention
to kick has been announced, the ball must be kicked. The
receiving team must have at least three men on the line of
scrimmage. Members of either team will not be permitted
to cross the line of scrimmage until the ball has been kicked.
If either team violates the rule before the ball has been
kicked, the offended team has the choice of calling the kick
over. The fumble rule does not apply to the kicking team
on a kick on the fifth down.

p. *Touchback.* A touchback occurs when the ball is declared dead in possession of a team behind its own goal line,
the impetus which caused the ball to cross the goal line having been given by the opposing team (e.g., intercepted
passes in end zone not returned to field of play, punts received in end zone not returned to field of play, all kicks
by attacking team going out of bounds in end zone or over
end line). After a touchback, the team making it shall put
the ball in play by scrimmage anywhere on its own 10-yard
line. A forward pass incomplete in the opponents' end zone
on the fifth down is not a touchback. The ball goes to the
opponents at the spot of the previous down. (Intentionally
grounding the ball on the fifth down not only gives the ball

to the opponents from the spot it was put in play, but a 5-yard penalty is also exacted.)

q. *Safety*. A safety occurs when the ball is declared dead in possession of the offensive team behind its own goal line, the impetus which caused the ball to be dead having been given by that team (e.g., kicks blocked going out of bounds in own end zone or over end line, fumble in own end zone by team putting ball in play, grounded pass from center in own end zone). The score for a safety is 2 points. The ball is put in play by a free kick on the 10-yard line, the same as a kickoff.

r. *Huddle*. 20 seconds will be allowed in a huddle.

Penalty. Loss of 5 yards.

s. *Tie Games*. If a tie game exists at the end of the regular playing time, the winner shall be determined through an extra series of plays. To begin the extra period, the ball shall be placed in the center of the field and a coin tossed to decide which team shall have the choice of goal or of initiating the series of offensive plays. Each team will have four plays, alternating possession of the ball after each play. The team in whose territory the ball is resting at the end of the eight-play series will be declared the loser, the opposing team receiving one point and being declared the winner. (NOTE: During this extra series of plays, an intercepted pass is the same as an incomplete pass on the fifth down.)

Should a team score before the eight-play series is completed, the contest continues, with teams alternating in possession of the ball until each side has had its four downs. The scoring play counts as one play in the series and the ball is returned to the midfield for the next play.

No kicking, except try-for-point after touchdown, will be permitted in the extra period games. After each play the ball shall be placed halfway between the sidelines in line with the spot where the ball was declared dead.

There shall be no time outs, except in case of injury, which will be at the discretion of the referee. The penalty for attempting to delay the game by faking an injury shall be loss of 15 yards.

First United States Army Flag Football Rules

1. For information and guidance of all concerned, flag football competition will be conducted in accordance with NCAA Football Rules, with the following changes or exceptions:

a. Uniform.

(1) All players will be dressed uniformly.

(2) Players of opposing teams must wear jerseys of contrasting colors.

(3) All players must wear shorts, sweat pants, fatigue pants, or football pants without hip and thigh pads.

(4) Basketball-type shoes or rubber-soled rubber-cleated athletic shoes may be worn. (Football shoes are not authorized.) Each team is urged to have the rubber-cleated athletic shoes.

(5) The flag to be used shall be a strip of canvas, twill cloth, plastic, or other strong material, approximately three inches wide and twenty inches long. Two flags will be a part of the uniform of each player, and opposing teams must wear flags of contrasting colors. Colors shall be red, white, blue, or gold. A commercial belt-type flag may be used.

(6) One flag will be tucked inside the pants on each hip at the outseam of the pants. Approximately five

inches of each flag will be tucked inside the trousers with approximately fifteen inches exposed.

(7) Wrapping, tying, or securing the flag to the trousers and/or belt is unsportsmanlike conduct and will be penalized accordingly.

(8) Protective equipment other than supporters, knee and ankle braces will not be worn.

b. Length of Game.

The game will be played in four periods, each ten minutes long, with one minute between quarters and ten minutes between halves.

c. Players and Substitutions.

(1) Players—A team shall consist of seven players. The offensive team must have at least three men on the line of scrimmage when the ball is snapped. The defensive team must have at least three men between 10 and 15 yards from the offensive team's restraining line on the kickoff.

(2) Substitutions—Unlimited substitutions may be made, except when the ball is in actual play.

d. Playing Regulations.

(1) Putting the ball in play—There will be one kickoff unless the ball does not go 10 yards, or a foul is involved. If the ball goes out of bounds regardless of touching or muffing, or untouched by the receiving team, it will be put in play on the receiving team's 40-yard line. If the ball goes more than 10 yards and goes out of bounds before reaching the receiver's 40-yard line, it will be put in play on the inbound spot. A kickoff not traveling 10 yards and recovered by the kicking team will be kicked over with a 5-yard penalty.

(2) Kicks—Any kick going over the opponent's

goal line without possession involved is dead—a touchback. This includes kickoffs.

(3) Fumbles and Muffs—Anytime the ball is fumbled or muffed during scrimmage, after lateral passing, a kick, a run, or pass from center, the ball belongs to the team first touching it after it hits the ground and it becomes dead at that spot. A ball passed from center which strikes the ground will be treated as a fumbled or muffed ball. This should eliminate diving at the ball. For the purpose of this rule, fumbling and muffing are considered the same.

(4) Blocking—In all instances, a blocker must be on his feet before and during contact with his opponent. The hands may not be in contact with the ground during a block. The block is executed in an upright or semi-upright position with contact only against the opponent's torso, arms or hands. Under no condition shall a high-low block be permitted.

Personal foul penalty—15 yards.

(Approved Ruling)—In the event a blocker makes legal contact and then loses footing or balance, and in the process of falling he makes contact below the opponent's hips; this will not be interpreted as a foul unless the blocker continues to drive forward into the opponent below the hips, in which case it is a foul.

(5) Downed Ball—The ball is downed and becomes dead when an opposing player pulls one of the flags from the runner. The player who removes the flag from the ball carrier should immediately hold the flag above his head at the spot when the capture was made.

(6) Passing—(a) All players of the offensive and defensive teams are eligible to receive passes.

(b) The receiver of a punt or free kick

may pass the ball forward provided he catches the ball before it strikes the ground and he does not take more than 2 steps after the catch except following a fair catch.

e. Fouls and Penalties.

(1) Tackling—It shall be a foul to tackle, hold, or rough another player. Personal foul penalty—loss of 15 yards by offensive player—15 yards by defensive player.

(2) Blocking—It shall be a foul to leave the feet or to block below the hips in an attempt to block an opponent. Personal foul penalty—loss of 15 yards.

(3) Personal Foul—The foul will be measured from the more severe spot on running plays. If the foul occurs in front of the ball, the penalty will be enforced from the ball. If the foul occurs behind the ball, the penalty will be enforced from that spot. On all running plays, fouls by defense will be penalized from where the run ends. On kicks, passes, etc., spot of enforcement will be from previous spot, except when foul is by offensive player behind the spot of snap, which will be from spot of foul.

f. Tie Games.

(1) In case of a tie game, each team will be given one series of downs in the same direction starting at the 50-yard line.

(2) The referee shall toss a coin in the presence of the two captains. The captain winning the toss shall have the choice of putting the ball in play first or last.

(3) The direction will be determined by mutual agreement of the two team captains, or by the referee if agreement cannot be reached.

(4) Play for the overtime period shall start within two minutes of the end of the fourth period.

(5) A series interrupted by a change of possession, or score, shall be considered a completed series.

(6) On change of possession during a down, the ball will continue in play until declared dead by an official in accordance with regular rules, and the point of gain for the team that put the ball in play will be the dead ball spot.

(7) Penalties shall be interpreted according to the regular rules under which the first four periods were played.

(8) The team gaining the most total yardage or points scored, including penalties, shall be awarded the win, based on points scored, or one point, in the event no points were scored.

Nine-Man Touch: as Played at the University of Oklahoma

1. A team shall consist of nine men—all eligible for pass.
2. Five men must be on the line of scrimmage on offense. Penalty 5 yards.
3. The game shall consist of four 10-minute quarters, 1-minute intermission between first and second, and third and fourth quarters. Five minutes between second and third quarters.
4. Time out is as follows: When the referee or captain calls time out; after a score is made; at the discretion of the referees; if too much time is consumed in inflicting a penalty; in making substitutions, etc. Time is in when the ball is actually put in play.
5. A team may have three official time outs during the game. Excess time-out penalty is 5 yards.
6. In place of being tackled, the ball carrier must be tagged with one hand below the head. In making the tag, both hands must be open. If foul occurred back

of the line of scrimmage, the penalty shall be from the spot where the ball was last put in play. Penalty 15 yards for tackling, 15 yards for unnecessary roughness in tagging. The player making the tag must have one foot on the ground at all times. Penalty 15 yards from spot of foul. Note: Holding the runner by the jersey or other parts of his clothing with one hand and tagging with the other hand is a foul. Penalty 15 yards from spot of foul. Any time a tag is made with unreasonable force, it shall be a 15-yard penalty and if flagrant, expulsion from the game. It shall be the same if the passer is blocked unreasonably hard. If the defensive player hits the passer in the head or face, it is a foul. 15-yard penalty.

7. Body blocking is not permitted under any circumstances. No downfield blocking three yards beyond the line of scrimmage. No man downfield may run into a man with his elbows extended. 15-yard penalty.

8. No player may use his hands on the head of opponent. Defensive players are restricted in the use of their hands to the shoulders and body of the offensive player. Penalty 15 yards. Any player who strikes a player on the head shall be disqualified from the game, and a penalty of 15 yards. This means either intentionally or unintentionally with either an elbow, hand, fist, or shoulder.

9. All men are eligible to receive a forward pass.

10. Penalty for incompleted forward pass, loss of a down.

11. When a man is tagged in the act of passing the ball it is dead at the spot of tagging, regardless of what follows.

12. Any time the ball is muffed or fumbled and touches the ground, the ball is dead, and belongs to the team that

muffed the ball at the spot it touched the ground. A blocked kick from scrimmage is dead when it touches the ground and shall belong to the defensive team at the spot where it was put in play. If the ball is centered over a player's head, it is dead at the point of contact with the ground. A muffed ball striking the ground always belongs to the team in possession of the ball unless it was fourth down, and the team failed to make its necessary yardage. A ball becoming dead behind one's own goal under this rule is an automatic safety. Note: If a ball from center hits the ground before being touched, it may be played, but if muffed or fumbled, it is dead at the spot it touches the ground.

13. The field shall be 50 yards wide and 80 yards long. It shall be laid off in zones 20 yards in width.

14. A team shall have four downs to advance the ball from one zone to another. If they fail to do so, they lose the ball to opponents at the spot.

15. The game shall start by putting the ball in play by scrimmage on the offensive team's 20-yard line. The same after a touchdown or safety with the team scored on taking the ball. A flip of a coin shall determine the choice of goal for the ball.

16. No runback on a punt. The ball is dead where caught and if not caught, where it rolls dead.

17. Any number of players may be substituted while the clock is running, if they do not delay getting the play-off in the regulation time (30 seconds).

18. The offensive team has 30 seconds from the time the referee puts the ball on the ground to run the next play. Penalty 5 yards.

19. No hideouts permitted. Penalty 5 yards. (Player must be in the huddle when the signal is called.)

20. A substitute must have on his jersey when coming in the game. Penalty 5 yards.

21. No time out allowed either team in last two minutes of second or fourth quarters except for injury.

22. Ball cannot be fumbled forward.

23. If the offensive team declares a kick, the defensive team may not rush. Offensive team has only 3 seconds to punt the ball. Penalty 5 yards.

24. A punted ball that is muffed or fumbled belongs to the team that muffed or fumbled it at the point it touches the ground.

25. Regular touch football rules shall govern if not covered by these rules.

26. Diagram chart cards may be used in calling signals.

27. Soft-soled shoes shall be worn. No cleated or spiked shoes, or any special protective devices such as shoulder pads, helmets, etc., shall be allowed.

28. Scoring touchdown, 6 points. Try after touchdown, 1 point. Safety, 2 points.

29. A penalty inside the 20-yard line may not be more than half the distance to the goal line.
    Supplemental touch football rules follow.

Supplemental Touch Football Rulings

1. It shall be the responsibility of all players regardless of whether they are on the offense or defense, to avoid contact that might injure a player.

2. If a man is going in to block a pass it is his responsibility to avoid contact with the passer with such force as to

injure him, regardless of whether the defensive man hits the ball or not.

3. If a ball carrier runs over the man trying to tag him without making any effort to avoid the tackler, this is unnecessary roughness, and a penalty of 15 yards, and, if flagrant, expulsion from the game. The use of a forearm block is flagrant, unnecessary roughness, and carries a 15-yard penalty and expulsion from the game.

4. A player expelled from two intramural games for roughness, fighting, or flagrant, unsportsmanlike conduct shall be barred from further competition in that sport for the rest of the season.

Note: If, in the opinion of the referee and the Intramural Faculty, the offense was malicious, the offender may be dropped from any further participation immediately without having the benefit of a second chance.

Tie-Game Ruling

If the games are tied at the end of regulation playing time, the penetration rule shall be used to determine the winner. A penetration shall be considered when the offensive team has the ball inside the opponent's 20-yard line. If the penetrations are even, then the following shall be used to break the tie. The officials shall then toss a coin and designate which field captain shall call; the winner of the toss shall have the choice of putting the ball in play or choice of goal, which choice shall not be revokable. The ball shall be placed in the center of the field and on the 40-yard line. Each team is given four plays, alternative in turn. The team that has scored the most points or has advanced the ball the farthest into the opponent's territory at the end of the eighth play is declared the winner. No punting is allowed during this period. In case either team scored a touchdown, the try for point is allowed to be played, and does not count as a down, and the ball is brought back to the center of the field and play resumed by scrimmage.

Rules for Instant Touch

Most of the rules drawn up by the colleges majoring in Touch are based upon current intercollegiate standards for regular football, and hence they are adaptations of a quite comprehensive and occasionally heavily populated process. To counteract such substantial but possibly dismaying advices in this book, here is a set of off-the-cuff rules boiling the whole thing down to run-of-the-mill rubrics which should serve Touch devotees on sward, strand, street, strip, or swale.

1. Pace off a field as nearly 80 yards in length and 40 yards wide as you can. Don't worry if you wind up 50 by 20. Mark the goal boundaries with handkerchiefs at the corners, if possible, and the sidelines with sticks, stones, chairs, or ashcans if you run out of handkerchiefs.

2. Use one handkerchief as a field marker to designate the 10 yards needed for a first down.

3. Sides must be equal in numbers. An odd man may serve as umpire for four downs, then alternate as replacement with one of the players. Or the team with the extra player may simply ask each one of its number to alternate in sitting out a down.

4. Sides line up with half of each team in the forward line, within two feet of the line. They may play in tight or spread formation as they elect.

5. Each team has four downs, or tries, in which to advance

the ball for a first down. If this is accomplished, four more downs are earned, and so on until the advance is either stopped or the goal line crossed for a score. On a short field you can allow four downs to score or give up the ball.

6. A touchdown earns six points.

7. There are four periods of play, timed at from 5 to 10 minutes each. (Optional: no timing is used, but 20 plays constitute each quarter. When this system is used, each team has five downs in which to score, and the ball goes over to the other team after the score, or after the five downs have elapsed.)

8. Three rest periods of 2 minutes each are allowed each team in each quarter. Additional time-outs are penalized 5 yards.

9. The team winning the toss gets a choice between carrying the ball or choosing which goal to defend. Teams change goals at the end of each quarter.

10. The ball is put in play by a punt or pass to the receiving team or it can be put in play around the 30-yard line of the team which has elected to "receive."

11. After each touchdown, the team scored on can either receive a punt or pass or put the ball in play on its own 30-yard line.

12. A ball out-of-bounds on the sideline is put back into play 15 yards in from the sideline.

13. A team may elect to punt on any down, but must announce the decision. Defenders may not rush the kicker, and must stay behind the "line" until the ball is kicked.

14. A ball kicked over the goal line goes over to the defending team and is put in play on its 20-yard line.

15. Any backfield player may run with the ball or forward pass from behind the safety "line." Any player on his

team may receive the pass. All players may lateral or back-pass at any time, or from any position on the field.

16. All players on both teams are eligible to intercept a pass and run with it.

17. One backfield player may be in motion before the ball is snapped. (This rule is optional, since a man in motion is a projectile capable of producing rugged impact play. Suggestion: permit man in motion only in game permitting blocking.)

18. Only standing blocks are permitted at any point on the field. (Optional rule: blocks are enjoyable if you enjoy running into people.)

19. The tag must be made with both hands at a point above the waist and below the neck.

20. The ball is dead when it touches the ground, or when the man carrying it touches the ground with any part of his body but his feet.

Penalties:

5 yards for offside.

5 yards for extra time-out.

20 yards for unnecessary roughness or interference with catching of pass other than knocking ball down to the ground or intercepting it.

10 yards for embracing rather than tagging female players.

5 yards for kicking handkerchief markers, or using them to wipe shoes, mop brow, or blow nose.

No penalty may bring the ball closer than 1 yard from the goal line.

BORROWER'S NAME

Frederic A. Birmingham   700

SIGNATURE

How to Succeed at Touch Football

SERIAL NO.

ORGANIZATION

DATE DUE	TITLE	DATE RETURNED